The HarperCollins Travel Guides

UTTARANCHAL
KUMAON & GARHWAL

The HarperCollins Travel Guides

UTTARANCHAL
KUMAON & GARHWAL

HarperCollins *Publishers* India
a joint venture with

New Delhi

First published in India in 2003 by
HarperCollins *Publishers* India
a joint venture with
The India Today Group

HarperCollins *Publishers*
1A Hamilton House Connaught Place, New Delhi 110001, India
77-85 Fulham Palace Road, London W6 8JB, United Kingdom
Hazelton Lanes, 55 Avenue Road, Suite 2900, Toronto, Ontario M5R 3L2
and 1995 Markham Road, Scarborough, Ontario M1B 5M8, Canada
25 Ryde Road, Pymble, Sydney, NSW 2073, Australia
31 View Road, Glenfield, Auckland 10, New Zealand
10 East 53rd Street, New York NY 10022, USA

Typeset in 8/10 Calisto
Nikita Overseas Pvt. Ltd.

Printed and bound at
Thomson Press (India) Ltd.

Contents

Introduction

This vast, vast land that is India extends from Himalayan heights to the deepest oceanic depths and, in between these two extremes, manages to fit in every kind of travel option imaginable. From mangroves, rainforests and jungles where peril lurks behind every bush, from shifting sands in deserts which change the landscape ever so often, from tropical islands bypassed by developers, from metropolises raucous with the dissonance of a million voices to silken stretches of beaches, the quiet hush of backwaters, the cool allure of tall mountains, temple towns by the side of holy rivers and cities that are veritable museums, India promises a travel package that frustrates as often as it fulfils, demands as much as it delights.

India is readily accessible to travellers of every hue and on every kind of allowance. Indian trains provide the cheapest transportation or the ultimate in luxury for those with heavier wallets. Air travel is restricted to the most popular destinations but bus services cover every nook and corner of the great Indian subcontinent. Hotel rooms can cost an arm and a leg or next to nothing. A hot meal and a warm welcome are available even in the most remote places and where nothing else works, the lure of lucre will. The enormous network of tourism offices, tour operators and travel agents goes a long way in simplifying the complexities of travel.

Despite this, India can be even the experienced traveller's nemesis unless of course he knows his way around. And since most travellers love to forge fresh tracks and explore new places, the going can get tough. Unless there is a guide book that covers the fundamentals of travel – where to go (and where not to), where to stop, where to stay, what to do and what not to – or a book that tells you how to do it with routes, itineraries, schedules and transportation tips. Which is where we come in – with a guide that gives both options but focuses on travel in one state or region at a time.

The State: The ideal way to handle India is to cut it to a manageable size. Hence the twenty-nine States and six Union Territories – each one of them with a culture, language, landscape, ambience and personality that is unique to it. Flip the pages of this guidebook for a quick introduction to this part of India, for the low-down on its interesting places, some cultural inputs and travel ideas plus inside information on the lesser-known destinations, the secret hideaways and out-of-sight treasures. The book also tells the active traveller – the adventure sports enthusiast, the angler, the trekker, the river rafter – what, where, when and how to do it and who to contact for a Forest Rest House or a fishing license.

The Trail: This book attempts to deliver the traveller to his chosen destination in the shortest and most scenic way with itineraries and routes marked on trails that explore the region they traverse.

While each trail is customized for those who prefer to drive, with routes, distances and time chalked out from the nearest metro or last railhead, it also tells you about the alternatives – the train, bus and air connections. The trail doesn't just make its way from Point A to Point B but offers endless possibilities for a hands-on experience of the neighbourhood it is passing through. Enroute destinations are accompanied by details of accommodation and sightseeing. Special attractions, fairs and festivals and unusual elements are featured in boxes within the main text (so you can't miss them). The trail follows an itinerary but does not subscribe to inflexible schedules – a holiday is about spontaneity and the trail wholeheartedly endorses any impulse that leads a traveller to stop and stare.

So there you have it – an Indian state decoded and demystified for the traveller, complete with directions et al and in as few words as possible.

UPDATES PLEASE

While every effort has been made to ensure that every place of tourist interest is covered and facts, phone numbers and addresses are accurate, we are human and therefore prone to err. If a mountain has moved, a river run dry, a destination missed, a hotel closed or a road blocked, please write to us, we'll check it out and add it in. Do remember, all schedules are subject to change, so double check close to the date of travel to avoid any inconvenience.

Uttaranchal Facts & Stats

FACTS

Climate

Uttaranchal has two separate terrains and so two distinct climates.

The Himalayan region has weather typical of alpine and sub-alpine climate, characterized by pleasant summers, short and steady monsoons and long winters with heavy snowfall. The summers are mild but the weather can and does change quite capriciously, should it rain or cloud over. As it is, the difference in day and night temperatures is quite dramatic – a warm, sunny day with temperature around 25°C can plunge to a frosty 7°C at night. Winter temperatures are more constant, they descend to sub-zero and stay there. Heavy fog, low temperatures and even lower visibility are familiar features of the winter season.

The plains are another story! Their climatic condition is very akin to the north Indian plains – long, endless tropical summers with temperatures around 40°C made even more unbearable by high humidity. Winters are intense, damp and cold with temperatures falling to 1°C at times.

Summer: March to June
Monsoon: June to mid-September
Winter: Mid-September to March

Dress Code

Dress to keep cool in the summer months when the heat and humidity levels peak in the plains and foothills of Uttaranchal. Light woollens provide adequate protection in the higher altitude areas in summers. Winter requirements are heavy to very heavy woollens everywhere from Dehradun to Nainital. High altitude apparel is needed for treks to the glaciers.

Good quality gear and equipment for trekking, mountaineering and skiing is available at very nominal rents with Garhwal Mandal Vikas Nigam.

Food

Highly nutritious, predominantly vegetarian cuisine based on the local produce of cereals, pulses, vegetables and fruits. Traditional Garhwali and Kumaoni cuisine specialities include such highs as Bhang ki chutney eaten with Ras, Gahed ki dal, Dal ke parathe, Chainsoo, Kafuli, Thechwani and Roat and Ursa. A local specialty to bring back is the famous 'Bal Mithai' – condensed milk squares coated with tiny white sugar balls. Non-vegetarian food is available in restaurants and dhabas but not in the vicinity of temple towns where alcohol is also prohibited. But not smoking – an unhealthy percentage of the population of Uttaranchal lights up, statutory warnings notwithstanding.

Home Cooked Remedies – Uttaranchal s panacea for chronic ailments!
Rhododendron Squash – Excellent for heart patients.
Gahed Dal Soup – Get rid of those recalcitrant kidney stones and say goodbye to diabetes.

Best Time

October to June
Plains and Foothills: Any time of the year
High Altitude Areas: April to October (except during the monsoons July/August)

Adventure Sports Season

Trekking: April to October
River Rafting: October to April
Angling: February to May, October to November
Mountaineering: April to November
Paragliding: September to December; March to June
Skiing: January to March

Banks

State Bank of India & Post Office in most places, even the small towns.

Bigger cities like Dehradun, Nainital and Udham Singh Nagar have branches of most nationalized banks as well as an odd international bank branch office.

Banking Hours:
Monday to Friday: 10:00 hrs to 17:00 hrs
Saturdays: 10:00 hrs to 12:00 hrs
Private banks may remain open up to 17:00 hrs on Saturdays also.
Holidays: Sundays and National Holidays

Photography

No photographs, please. Not of military installations, bridges and dams. Camera permits are mandatory within the Inner Line.

Permits

Indian nationals do not need permits for trekking/travelling in Uttaranchal except in Restricted or Protected Areas of Arwa Tal, Nanda Devi Sanctuary, Darma Valley, north of Badrinath, Kamet, Niti Ghati, Kalindi Khal (Uttarkashi) and Milam glacier. For trekking routes inside the Inner Line, an Inner Line Permit (ILP) is essential and should be obtained from the District Magistrate, Joshimath or the Ministry of Home Affairs (Foreigners Division, Lok Nayak Bhawan, Khan Market, New Delhi-110 003) at least four weeks before the date of the travel. Only group permits are issued and individual tourists are not allowed to travel in the restricted areas.

Foreign nationals are not permitted to cross the Inner Line

boundary. No special sanctions are required for treks within altitudes of 4900 m but treks in altitudes higher than 4900 m need prior authorization from the Indian Mountaineering Foundation (Indian Mountaineering Foundation, Benito Juarez Marg, Anand Niketan, New Delhi–110021 Tel: 011-22671211).

@ Useful Websites
www.journeymart.com
www.uttaranchaltourism.gov.in
www.tourismofindia.com
www.garhwaltourism.com
www. kmvn.org
www.gmvn.com

STATS

Date of Birth: 9.11.2000
Interim Capital: Dehradun
Neighbours: Uttar Pradesh, Himachal Pradesh, Haryana, Nepal & Tibet
Total Area: 51,125 sq km Mountains, hills & foothills and Terai and Bhabar plains
Hilly Area: 92.57%
Plains: 7.43%
Forest cover: 63%
Agriculture Area: 11%
Divisions: 2–Garhwal & Kumaon
Districts: 13
Garhwal: Chamoli, Dehradun, Haridwar, Pauri, Rudraprayag, Tehri Garhwal, Uttarkashi
Kumaon: Almora, Bageshwar, Champawat, Nainital, Pithoragarh, Udham Singh Nagar
Rivers: Yamuna (AKA Tons), Bhagirathi (AKA Bhilangna), Alaknanda (AKA Mandakini, Nandakini, Saraswati and Pindar), Ramganga, Kosi and Mahakali (AKA Saryu, Dauli, Goli)
Peaks: Nanda Devi (7816 m), Chaukhamba (7138 m), Satopanth (7075 m), Trisul (7045 m), Kedarnath (6940 m), Kamet (6883 m) and Neelkanth (6596 m)
Glaciers: Bandarpoonch (4442 m), Chorabari (3800 m), Dokriani (3800 m), Doonagiri (4240 m), Gangotri (4000-6900 m), Pindari (3532-4625 m), Sunderdhunga (6053 m), Satopnath, Bhagirathi-Khark (3820 m), Khatling (3717m), Nandadevi, Namik, Ralam, Milam (4242 m) and Mrigthuni (6856 m)
Wildlife Parks: Askot Sanctuary (Pithoragarh), Binsar Sanctuary (Binsar), Nanda Devi National Park, Rajaji National Park, Corbett National Park and Tiger Reserve, Gobind Wildlife Sanctuary (Uttarkashi), Kedarnath Sanctuary and Valley of Flowers
Population: 7 million
Languages: Garhwali, Kumaoni and Hindi
Literacy: 65%

Tourist Offices

Kumaon Mandal Vikas Nigam Limited (KMVN)
102 Indraprakash Building
21 Barakhamba Road
New Delhi
Tel: 011-23712246, 23319835

Fax: 011-23327713
Email: kmvn@yahoo.com

Kumaon Mandal Vikas Nigam Limited
Oak Park, Nainital – 263001
Tel: 05942-236209
Fax: 05942-236897

Garhwal Mandal Vikas Nigam Limited (GMVN)
102 Indraprakash Building
21 Barakhamba Road
New Delhi
Tel: 011-23350481
Fax: 011-23327713
Email: gmvn@nda.vsnl.net.in

Garhwal Mandal Vikas Nigam Limited
Survey Chowk, Dehradun–248001
Tel: 0135-2653309
Fax: 0135-2746847

Kumaon (Kumaon Mandal Vikas Nigam)
Tourist Officer
Tourist Office
Almora
Tel: 05962-230180

Tourist Officer
Tourist Office
Champawat

Tourist Officer
Tourist Office
Oak Park, Nainital
Tel: 05942-236356

Tourist Officer
Tourist Bureau
Pithoragarh
Tel: 25527

Garhwal (Garhwal Mandal Vikas Nigam)

Tourist Officer
Tourist Bureau
Pauri
Tel: 01368-22241

Tourist Officer
Tourist Bureau
Joshimath
Tel: 01389-22181

Tourist Officer
Tourist Bureau
Dehradun
Tel: 0135-2653217

Tourist Officer
Regional Tourist Office
Haridwar
Tel: 0135-2428686

Tourist Information Centre
Railway Station
Haridwar
Tel: 2427817

Tourist Officer
Tourist Bureau
Lalta Rao Bridge, Haridwar
Tel: 0135-2424240

O.S.D. Adventure Tourism
Tourist Office
Uttarkashi
Tel: 01374-2290

THE ROUTE TO UTTARANCHAL

Bus Services

Excellent bus services link the different destinations in Uttaranchal to major cities and towns in the neighbouring states of Delhi, Uttar Pradesh, Himachal Pradesh and Haryana. Private and state roadways operate deluxe (air conditioned), semi-deluxe and ordinary buses to Dehradun, Haridwar, Rishikesh, Joshimath, Uttarkashi, Nainital, Almora, Pithoragarh and Haldwani.

Within Uttaranchal, bus services operated by the two umbrella organizations for bus companies, the Garhwal Motor Owners Union (GMOU) and Kumaon Motor Owners Union (KMOU) take care of transportation in their respective districts.

Air Services

Uttaranchal has three functional airports at Jolly Grant in Dehradun, Phool Bagh in Pantnagar and Naini Saini in Pithoragarh with helipads at Gauchar, Ananda, Joshimath and Uttarkashi. However, air services are few and far between – limited to small aircraft operated by private airlines like Jagson Airlines. Currently, the only operational service is the tri-weekly one to Dehradun from Delhi.

Train Schedule

One of the most comfortable ways to travel in Indian conditions, bearing in mind that roads tend to deteriorate post monsoons (actually post anything!), is by train. The only drawback with train travel is that it has to be planned, (spontaneous, spur of the moment ideas fall flat on their faces) and reservations made in good time. In the case of Uttaranchal, trains will get one only so far. A predominantly mountainous terrain precludes train travel to most places in Uttaranchal – the closest railheads are at Dehradun, Rishikesh, Kotdwar, Ramnagar and Kathgodam. Dehradun and Kathgodam are the main railheads connected to Delhi, Lucknow, Mumbai and Kolkata.

Jagson Airlines	To Dehradun	To Delhi	Frequency
	Flt # 401 Departure: 12:10 hrs Arrival 13:00 hrs	Flt#402 Departure: 13:20 hrs Arrival: 14:10 hrs	Mondays Wednesdays and Fridays

Train	From	Destination	Departure	Arrival	Frequency
# 2017 Shatabdi	New Delhi	Dehradun	07:00 hrs	12:40 hrs	Daily
#2018	Dehradun	Delhi	17:00 hrs	22:30 hrs	
#2055 Janshatabdi	New Delhi	Dehradun	15:30 hrs	21:10 hrs	Except on Sundays
#2056	Dehradun	Delhi	05:10 hrs	11:05 hrs	
#4041 Mussoorie Express	Delhi	Dehradun	22:15 hrs	08:00 hrs	Daily
#4042	Dehradun	Delhi	22:15 hrs	07:00 hrs	
# 9019 Dehradun Express	Mumbai	Dehradun	22:25 hrs	16:50 hrs	Daily
#9020	Dehradun	Mumbai	10:35 hrs	04:35 hrs	
#9265 Uttaranchal Express	Dwarka	Dehradun	12:20 hrs	19:00 hrs	Fridays
#9266	Dehradun	Dwarka	06:00 hrs	17:08 hrs	
# 3009 Doon Express	Howrah Junction	Dehradun (via Lucknow)	20:35 hrs	06:45 hrs	Daily
#3010	Dehradun	Howrah Jn	20:25 hrs	06:55 hrs	
#5013 Ranikhet Express	Delhi	Kathgodam	20:35 hrs	06:15 hrs	Daily
#5014	Kathgodam	Delhi	20:45 hrs	04:45 hrs	
#3019 Bagh Express	Howrah Jn	Kathgodam (via Lucknow)	21:45 hrs	08:45 hrs	Daily
#3020	Kathgodam	Howrah Jn	19:40 hrs	11:15 hrs	

Uttaranchal – Heaven on Earth

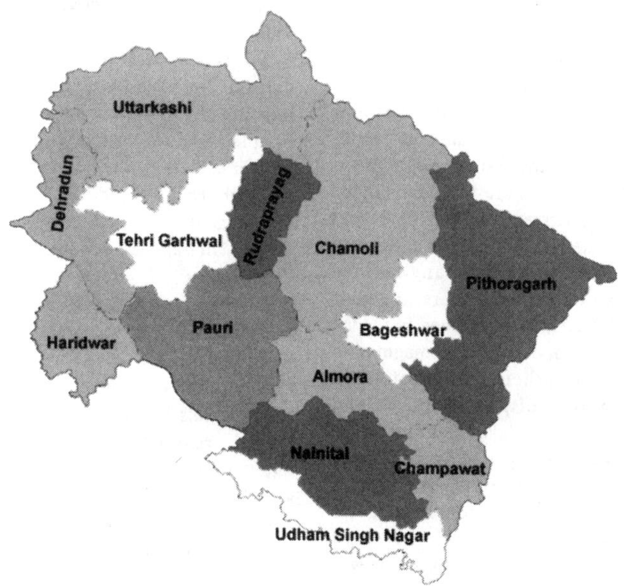

When Lord Brahma created the Hindu universe, he, sensibly, reserved a sizeable wedge of its most beautiful part for his fellow gods. Since then, the region we now call Uttaranchal has been revered as Dev Bhoomi, the Abode of Gods. And who other than the gods deserve to dwell in these Olympian heights, this heaven on earth where towering mountains look down upon miles of glaciers, frosted snowfields, vigorous rivers, alpine meadows, river sculpted valleys, dense forests and flower-sprinkled hillsides.

Were they gods of any other religion, lesser mortals would fear to venture near their homes, but Hindu gods share a deeply symbiotic relationship with their devotees and expect them to come visiting – once in a lifetime or as often as possible. So in the eons before travel became a leisure activity, all journeys to modern Uttaranchal were yatras – pilgrimages to pay homage to the gods. And to ensure their devotees came again and again, the gods created several venerated pilgrimage sites scattered across the length and breadth of the Himalayas, first by way of Mt Swargarohini (6252 m) in western Garhwal.

The history of the region is milestoned, not by tangible events, but by myths and legends – this is after all the land of gods peopled by mystics and mysterious beings like the Nagas, a tribe that claimed descent from the many-hooded King of Serpents. Here, the gods indulged in power games, tested the believer and taxed the imagination of the atheist; they donned disguises, displayed moods and deified rocks, lakes and mountains till every little patch of land became sanctified. This was where mystics defied the elements in their determination to resolve philosophical conundrums or win the favours of the gods and this was the place that Shiva harnessed the vigour of the River Ganga, only to release her in multiple manageable streams.

As evident, this is no ordinary land – it is a place of gods and goddesses, celestial beings and sages, fables and folklore, a place of such rare beauty that even its most cynical visitor undergoes a transcendental experience.

Uttaranchal's recent history has been infinitely more fraught as its people fought off armed aggression from outside and cultural invasion from inside. Local kingdoms collapsed and foreigners ruled till they were deposed by time and events. The Uttaranchal we see today is the result of a long struggle to preserve natural resources and cultural heritage by achieving a measure of regional autonomy. The people won the day when in November 2000, their homeland was reborn as the new state of Uttaranchal.

New Uttaranchal is composed of vast tracts of predominantly mountainous terrain cordoned by the Himalayas in the north, the River Tons in the west, River Kali Ganga in the east and foothills of the Shivaliks in the south. India's most revered and most indispensable rivers – the Yamuna and Ganga – were born in the glaciers and snowfields of the Himalayas and on their way down to the plains create deep gorges and sculpt fertile valleys.

The two regions of Garhwal and Kumaon make up Uttaranchal. Garhwal, more robust and generously proportioned, spreads towards the northwest while Kumaon, small, delicate and beautiful, lies to the east. Outstanding in appearance, both rival each other's beauty as silent glaciers, jagged peaks, quartz and granite ridges, forested slopes, alpine lakes, fast flowing rivers and countless cascading waterfalls contribute to their glory.

GARHWAL – LAND OF FORTS

Garhwal consists almost entirely of rugged mountains, high altitude areas separated by narrow valleys or deep gorges through which race the torrential waters of the Rivers Yamuna, Bhagirathi, Alaknanda, Mandakini, Dhauli Ganga, and Pindar. It gets its name from the fact that once upon a time, the region was a seething mass of little princedoms defined by small fortresses or garhs. At last count, 52 small chieftains had carved up the territory between themselves, each lord of his own private garh!

With so many fractious factions at work, Garhwal was an object of desire irresistible to neighbouring kings who repeatedly sent troops to annexe both land and people. Sometimes they succeeded as in the case of the Gurkhas of Nepal (1803-04) and sometimes they didn't, as happened to the forces of the Mughal Emperor Shah Jehan (1640). The Garhwalis were so utterly miserable during the Gurkha rule that they happily signed away a large portion of their land, including Dehradun and Pauri, in exchange for British assistance.

Garhwal includes the districts of Chamoli, Dehradun, Haridwar, Pauri, Rudraprayag, Tehri Garhwal and Uttarkashi. Within these districts fall some of Uttaranchal's most popular destinations – the holy cities of Haridwar and Rishikesh, the ultra sacred Char Dham (Yamunotri, Gangotri, Kedarnath and Badrinath); the Panch Prayags (Devaprayag, Rudraprayag, Karnaprayag, Nandprayag and Vishnuprayag), the Panch Badris, the exquisite Valley of Flowers, hill resorts like Mussoorie, Dhanaulti, Chakrata and Chopta; adventure sports centres like Auli, Joshimath and Okhimath and Dehradun – the interim capital of Uttaranchal.

Bloody nose
Queen Karnavati of Garhwal personally led her troops against the might of the Mughal forces and defeated them. Not satisfied with a figurative bloody nose, she decided they deserved a literal one too – so she ordered her men to cut off the noses of all the poor POWs. Her version of a victory lap earned the Queen the sobriquet of Nak-Katti Rani – Queen who cut noses!

Chamoli

Sitting squarely in the middle of Uttaranchal is Chamoli, a district spreading over some 7520 sq km crisscrossed by several important rivers and their tributaries including the powerful Alaknanda, Saraswati, Bhagirathi, Dhauli Ganga, Nandakini and Pindar, to name just a few.

Spiritually well endowed, Chamoli district is full of holy sites visited by thousands of pilgrims each year. Actually, Chamoli, more than any other district, is the domain of Lord Shiva – the divine architect who masterminds the cosmic cycle of destruction and recreation and has hundreds of shrines dedicated to him, the most important being Badrinath. Others on the list of the many temples and shrines spread around these beautiful mountains include Hemkund Sahib, Kalpeshwar, Rudranath, Tungnath, three of the Panch Badris and two Panch Prayags.

For the less religiously inclined traveller, Chamoli offers myriad opportunities – whether it be the breathtaking beauty of the Valley of Flowers or the heart-stopping excitement of river rafting down the Alaknanda, skiing in Auli or simply exhaling in wonder at the splendid vista of the Himalayas as seen from Gopeshwar, Chopta, Tapovan and Pipalkoti.

Hug a tree to save the tree

The Chipko Andolan, a 1970s grassroots movement to conserve the remaining forests of Uttaranchal, was born in Chamoli under the aegis of Gandhians, Sunderlal Bahuguna and Chandi Prasad Bhatt. Activists for the movement fanned out across the Garhwal and Kumaon Hills spreading the message of conservation and inspiring local communities to take on the combined might of state government, commercial loggers and development planners. Ordinary women were at the forefront of this nonviolent movement, and were prepared to lay down their lives embracing a tree rather than let it be cut down. Their courage and determination was rewarded by a total ban on tree felling above 1000 metres in 1980.

Dehradun

The interim capital of Uttaranchal needs no introduction – it has long been a popular enroute stop if not the end destination for those escaping the sweltering heat of north Indian summers. Once a small garrison town with excellent educational institutions, it was top of the list of those planning a comfortable retirement, not far from Delhi but not too close either. Not anymore because today Dehradun flaunts its newly acquired eminence with inflation, escalating prices of real estate and roads crowded with self-important white Ambassadors flashing lights – the omnipresent and unmistakeable symbols of government.

Despite the paraphernalia of administration, those that Doon captivates are hooked forever by the slow pace of life, the clear, clean air and its old world ambience. Numbered amongst Doon delights is the vast estate at Hathibarkala housing the Survey of India, the green wonderland of the Forest Research Institute, the spit and polish of the Indian Military Academy, India's Eton, the Doon School, and the notable main thoroughfare, Rajpur Road, with its eating places, hotels, confectionary shops and bakeries. Beyond Dehradun's city limits lie numerous charming getaways and picnic spots – Sahastradhara, Dak Pathar, Rajaji National Park, Malsi Deer Park, Doiwala and Robber's Cave.

As Rajpur Road pulls away from the chaos and congestion of its busiest stretch, it heads towards the Queen of the Hills, Mussoorie. At night, Mussoorie's lights twinkle in the darkness like a galaxy of stars close enough to touch and their allure is so irresistible that just about everyone who visits Dehradun has to travel the intermediate 34 km to Mussoorie. Mussoorie is an invitation to do nothing more strenuous than long walks through pine-scented forests, indolent picnics in flower-filled meadows, pony rides or swapping ghost stories over long drinks by blazing fires.

To the northwest of Dehradun is Chakrata, another charming Garhwali hill town, not half as well developed as Mussoorie but then not as well visited either. Chakrata's appeal lies in its promise of serenity, tranquility and solitude. Basically a cantonment town where the olive green uniform of the Indian Army

Mussoorie's celeb list – past and present

Pahadi Wilson – business baron and sire of many of Mussoorie's fair-skinned, blue-eyed natives.

Ruskin Bond – Storyteller and chronicler of Mussoorie.

Victor Banerjee – Gentleman actor and Oscar nominee.

Hugh & Colleen Gantzer – Travellers and writers extraordinaire.

has ensured the forests of deodar, conifers and oak are off limits to loggers and developers, Chakrata retains a fair bit of the colonial aura, especially in the British era barracks, buildings, cemetery and check posts. Though visitors to Chakrata are more likely to encounter smiling Tibetan faces than stern British visages!

The mountainscape over Mussoorie and Chakrata is great trekking country – Deoband, Tyuni, Purola, Har ki Doon, Yamunotri, Banderpoonch Glacier, Dodi Tal, Nag Tibba and Dhanaulti are just some of the destinations that offer challenging treks.

Haridwar

Hinduism's gateway to the gods – the one pilgrimage that most pious Hindus manage to make, posthumously if not in life! Haridwar and Rishikesh, the other holy town on the banks of the Ganga, have been venerated for as long as Hindus can remember. Both places are packed with temples, ashrams, dharamshalas and gurukuls and their workforce – priests, sadhus, swamis, gurus and students.

In recent times, travellers other than pilgrims have also been heading for Haridwar and Rishikesh, lured by the area's immense potential for adventure sports and leisure activities. At Rishikesh, the Ganga's headlong descent is abruptly slowed creating the perfect white water at Shivapuri, Kaudilya and Byasi for river rafting. As the gradient gets gentler, the river becomes calmer and is ideal for kayaking and canoeing.

Encampments along the banks of the Ganga provide excellent facilities for water sports, hot air ballooning, camping and trekking in the surrounding wilderness.

Pauri

Outstanding views of the snow bound Himalayas on the one hand, and a multi-hued patchwork quilt in the valley below with meandering rivers and thick tracts of forests on the other – that is what Pauri has to offer. The district of Pauri Garhwal begins in the foothills of the fertile Bhabar area of Kotdwar (395 m, the nearest railhead) and stretches upwards to the high altitude pastureland around Dudhatoli (3100 m). In between these altitudes are innumerable attractive spots – Lansdowne, Adwani, Kanva Ashram, Binsar, Khirsu, Kalagarh, Sainji, Thalisain and Tara Kund – well equipped with GMVN Tourist Rest Houses and small hotels for that quiet holiday.

Pauri also has plenty for the active traveller in search of action – treks to Binsar, Dudhatoli, Gairsain, Markhal Pass and Tara Kund; aero sports at Kandara near Kotdwar, angling for Mahseer in the Nayyar River at Satpuli as well as cycling, camping and rock climbing. (For details contact Coordinator, Adventure Activities Cell, Department of Tourism, PO Box-33, HNB Garhwal University, Srinagar, Garhwal – 246 174. Tel: 01388-251051.)

Pauri's next-door neighbours are the two national parks – Chilla Wildlife Sanctuary (Rajaji National Park) and Corbett Tiger Reserve with a good complement of tigers, elephants, deer, nilgai, bears, monkeys, crocodiles and jungle fowl.

Rudraprayag

A region of immense natural beauty replete with the bounty of glaciers, mountains, ferocious rivers, alpine lakes and a lush valley. The district is named after Shiva in his Rudra avatar – legend has it that the Lord appeared as Rudra to bless Narada Muni's quest to master the intricacies of music thus ensuring that Narada became the repository of Indian classical music.

Located at the confluence of the Rivers Alaknanda and Mandakini as they descend at a fast and furious pace from their respective sources at Kedarnath and Badrinath, Rudraprayag is venerated as one of the five sacred confluences, the Panch Prayags. However, the most revered site in the district is the shrine at Kedarnath – the mountain abode of Lord Vishnu at the foot of Mt Kedarnath in the snowfields of the Gangotri Glacier.

Sitting at the tri-junction of three beautiful districts of Chamoli, Uttarkashi and Tehri, Rudraprayag is ideally situated for pilgrimages to Kedarnath, Badrinath, and Gangotri. For the most part, the roads leading to these districts run parallel to the Rivers Mandakini, Alaknanda and Pindar, making it one of the most scenic places in Uttaranchal. Within Rudraprayag, the places worth checking out are the picturesque towns of Tilwara, Agustmuni, Guptkashi, Sonprayag, Okhimath, Vasuki Tal, Deoria Tal and Gandhi Sarovar.

In common with other places in Garhwal, Rudraprayag too offers ample opportunities for adventure sports like trekking, mountaineering, river rafting and angling. Accommodation, too, is available in plenty – modestly priced lodges, GMVN Tourist Rest Houses and deluxe resorts.

Tehri Garhwal

Lying across the southern slopes of the Outer Himalayas, Tehri extends its dominion from the peaks of the Gangotri group all the way down to Rishikesh. The district has a long and hoary history mostly because it was the heart of the once powerful kingdom of Tehri-Garhwal before the Gurkhas' invasions forced the king to cede parts of his empire to the British. The district is located in a wide valley filled with forests of birch and pine, fed by the waters of the River Bhagirathi hurtling down from its source in Gangotri. So powerful are the torrents of the Bhagirathi that they nearly rip the district asunder in their tearing hurry to get to the plains.

Old Tehri, on the confluence of the Bhagirathi and Bhilangna, met its watery end in the swirling waters of the controversial Tehri Dam and its residents rehabilitated in the spanking new township 25 km downhill. Well connected by road to Dehradun, Rishikesh, Mussoorie, Pauri and Uttarkashi, the district's prettiest places are Chamba, Dhanaulti and Narendra Nagar.

Uttarkashi

Uttarkashi, district headquarters and temple town on the banks of the Bhagirathi, is considered to have the same religious consequence as Kashi or Varanasi. Shiva is the presiding deity enshrined in the Vishwanath temple (that's how seriously they take the Varanasi analogy). Other important temples are dedicated to Parshurama, Ekadash Rudra and Kali.

Lying on the main route to the shrine of Gangotri, Uttarkashi has been an important stopover for pilgrims trekking their way up to the source of the River Ganga. In recent times, the newfound enthusiasm for adventure sports has made Uttarkashi an even more popular destination, mainly because it houses the prestigious Nehru Institute of Mountaineering, the Mecca of Indian mountaineering. NIM offers short and long term courses in basic and advance mountaineering, rock climbing, trekking, bush craft and adventure courses. Consequently, Uttarkashi has a large number of hotels and lodges catering to the heavy traffic of pilgrims, tourists and mountaineers.

Uttarkashi is the base for some of the toughest treks in Garhwal – the ones to be undertaken by experienced trekkers only are treks to the glaciers at Gaumukh, Gangotri and Khatling, and the relatively softer treks to Dayara Bugyal, Dodi Tal, Shasra Tal, Khara Tal and Masap Tal.

Garhwal: Cultural Insights

* The groom has to bear the financial burden of the wedding ceremony and feast – if he doesn't have the necessary funds, he either remains single or earns himself a spouse by working for his father-in-law.
* The Dhurang dance is performed by the Bhotiya tribe to release the soul of a dead Bhotiya, which would otherwise remain trapped in the body of a goat or some other animal.
* Rifleman Jaswant Singh of the 4th Garhwal Rifles gave up his life defending an outpost on the Indo-Chinese border, 40 years ago. The soldier has been promoted regularly since then, as if he was still on active duty and now wears the rank of a Major General.

KUMAON – LAND OF THE TORTOISE

Kumaon derives its name from Lord Vishnu who appeared in Champawat in his incarnation as a tortoise – part of an ongoing process under which Vishnu, the Preserver of the Hindu Trinity, is reborn in different incarnations or avatars to save the universe from catastrophe.

Whereas Garhwal is rugged and tough, sanctified with endless numbers of holy sites and sculpted by turbulent rivers that power their way down craggy mountain terrain, Kumaon has the gentler mien of a younger sibling, a quiet beauty that is as captivating as Garhwal's macho mountainscape. If Garhwal beckons the spiritual traveller then Kumaon is the vacation specialist, the place for leisurely holidays spent in the midst of pine forests, fruit orchards, mountain lakes and gentle rolling hills.

Kumaon isn't all that big in terms of area (21,035 sq km) and would have grown were it not squashed into a corner by Garhwal from the west, the Mahakali River from the east and the uncompromising Himalayas in the north – that left Kumaon no place to go except south where it met up with the fertile alluvial plains of the Terai region. What it lost in size, Kumaon provides in magnificence – there is possibly no other region as idyllic as Kumaon with its snow-clad mountains (Nanda Devi, Kailash, Panchchhuli, Trishul), crystalline lakes, prolific valleys and hillsides covered with lacy ferns and slender conifers. This abundance of natural beauty is enlivened by the presence of temple towns with a hoary past, hill resorts ready for summer visitors and forests that are as rich in fauna as they are in fables and stories.

Kumaon was ruled by the powerful Katyuri and Chand dynasties that were between them responsible for the exquisite temple complexes at Baijnath, Jageshwar and Katarmal. The Katyuri kings ruled Kumaon, Garhwal and parts of western Nepal during the Medieval Period (7th-11th century AD) when the Chands of Pithoragarh displaced them. The Chands were great, innovative builders who left the fabulous 164 temple complex at Jageshwar as a testament to their times.

The British 'discovered' Kumaon in the early 1820s when some intrepid Englishmen began to explore the hilly tracts edging the plains of north India. And it is the British we need to thank for 'hill stations' – those quintessential colonial hand-me-downs that were the result of desperate efforts to escape the heat – like Nainital and Ranikhet. There are many interesting versions doing the rounds that tell us how the British actually got their hands on the best real estate in Kumaon. One version narrates how an Englishman took the village headman for a sail in what is now Naini Lake. Fully cognizant of the fact that the headman didn't know how to swim, the Englishman threatened to tip the boat over unless the poor fella signed over all his land to Company Bahadur – the East India Company. Fearing for his life, the headman did so and thus, the British gained land rights to prime property.

Kumaon consists of the six districts of Almora, Bageshwar, Champawat, Nainital, Pithoragarh and Udham Singh Nagar. Each of these districts is a destination by itself offering a variety of experiences for both the indolent and the active traveller.

The Raj's 'Hill Station' Ethos

Homes away from home, the British visualized and built them to bear as close a resemblance to Mother England as possible. They all had the essential English architectural landmarks –a church, a central avenue for walks or rides (always called The Mall!) and a clubhouse. Those who came up for the summer had truly arrived and those who owned homes here were even more superior. And finally, hill stations were the breeding ground of future generations of the ruling class, that is why there are so many residential schools in 'hill stations'.

Almora

Perched on a saddle shaped ridge above the Rivers Kosi and Suyal, Almora offers panoramic views of the Himalayan ranges from almost everywhere. An extremely invigorating climate and lack of bright lights have been Almora's main draw – which is why the British considered it the perfect place for a spot of rest and recuperation.

Established in the second half of the 16th century, Almora was the capital of the Katyuri kings before it passed into the control of the Chand dynasty of Pithoragarh. Under their guidance, Almora became the repository for Kumaoni culture, a heritage still preserved in folk songs and dances, crafts, costumes, cuisine and in the wooden carvings used to decorate homes.

Almora is often referred to as the 'city of temples' – as are many other cities in India – but Almora owes this cachet to the ancient Nanda Devi Temple that sits square in the centre of town. Other important temples in the vicinity include the famous Chitai Temple dedicated to Gollu Dev, Kasar Devi temple at Kalimatt, the 800-year-old Sun Temple at Katarmal, Shiva temples at Binsar and Gannath and the incredible temple complex at Jageshwar.

The district's most popular resorts are at Ranikhet, Binsar, Chaukori and Kausani. Each one of them has the uncanny ability to hook the first time visitor and leave him enthralled for life. Ranikhet is a quintessential cantonment town that retains its colonial ambience, kept alive by the men in olive green. The credit for keeping Ranikhet green and clean is also theirs. The Binsar Sanctuary spreads around the town almost enfolding it in a deeply wooded embrace. Great views, solitude and scenic splendours, that's Binsar's secret recipe for a terrific holiday. Kausani is, of course, India's answer to Switzerland. Even Mahatma Gandhi thought so – after he spent 12 whole days in this quiet little hamlet that offers fabulous views of Mts Nanda Devi and Trishul.

Prehistoric Almora

Three important prehistoric sites dating to the Bronze-Stone Age have been found around Almora at Lakhuudiyar (20 km), Pharkanauli and Phulseema (4 km). The rock paintings at Lakhuudiyar on the banks of the River Suyal are of men and animals – groups of dancers, lizards, deer and so on – while those at Phulseema and Pharkanauli are less clear, more a series of red lines representing human figures doing different actions.

Bageshwar

On the confluence of the Rivers Saryu, Gomti and Bhagirathi lies Bageshwar – a town with strong association with Shiva. So strong that a dip in its waters or a pilgrimage to its Shiva Temple is enough to liberate a good Hindu from the eternal cycle of birth and death. Bageshwar is doubly blessed, by the Lord's presence and by scenic surroundings – the Nileshwar and Bhileshwar Ranges are its guardian angels watching over its hallowed land.

The high altitude areas beyond Bageshwar are a trekker's delight with different routes leading to the glaciers of Pindari, Namik, Sunderdhunga and Nandakot. The trail to Pindari Glacier follows the Pindar River to its source at the base of Mts Nandakot (6,860 m), Chhanguch (6322 m) and Nandaghunti (6310 m). Further ahead, to the east and west of Pindari Glacier are the Kaphni, Namik and Sunderdhunga Glaciers. Bageshwar offers pastoral interludes at Baijnath, Gwaldam, Berinag and Kausani – places close by for travellers looking for less taxing holidays – in GMVN and KMVN Tourist Rest Houses and lodges.

Champawat

Equally famed for its ancient temples and monuments as it is for its natural beauty, Champawat was the capital of the once-powerful Chand dynasty. Champawat would have sunk into oblivion with the collapse of their kingdom were it not catapulted into literary history thanks to the man-eating tiger who lived off the villagers! It needed a hunter of the calibre of Jim Corbett to despatch the tiger and write its epitaph in the best selling 'Man Eater of Champawat'.

Champawat owes much to Jim Corbett whose writings inspired many an Englishman and Indian to head for its densely forested hills – some came for short sojourns, others created little settlements like Abbot Mount from where they could look up at the snow-clad summits peeping out from behind cotton wool clouds or look down upon a valley full of forests, fields, flowers and fruit trees.

Call for Corbett
For 35 years starting from 1906, Jim Corbett hunted down tigers – notching his last kill at the age of 63. Each time a tiger switched his diet from venison to men, out went the call for Corbett Sahib and Corbett Sahib responded by first banishing all other hunters from the area. He would then set traps, beat around the bush and trick the man-eater out with mating calls and tasty morsels before sending him/her off to the tiger's Valhalla.

Nainital

In recent years Nainital has been written more on account of its dying lake than for its scenic wonders. True, Naini Lake is embattled from within and without – unrestricted construction has caused such severe erosion that the silt build-up is choking the lake – but it still remains Kumaon's crown jewel! Naini Lake glitters like a jewel in emerald green setting, (now sadly more brown than green), the Mall prospers off the thousands of summer visitors and the hotel rooms in Nainital still need to be booked in advance.

Nainital is often called Kumaon's Lake District and it certainly has the class and numbers to qualify as one. Sapphire blue, aquamarine and emerald green lakes lying scattered around like so many gemstones sparkle against the dense green of conifer, oak and deodar clad hills. Bhim Tal, Khurpa Tal, Naukuchiya Tal and Sat Tal – each one of them supports a small town or village that offers modest accommodation and adequate facilities for boating or angling.

Also falling within Nainital's district limits is the Corbett National Park located in the terai region and straddling the rolling Shivalik foothills. Established in 1936 on the advise of Jim Corbett, the park houses over 50 mammal, 600 bird and 25 reptile species apart from the Indian tiger.

Pithoragarh

Tucked so high and so deep in the Himalayans that only those aware of the raw, unfettered beauty of these majestic mountains actually travel to Pithoragarh. A majority of its first-time visitors come here by the way! Pithoragarh figures on the route maps of those heading for magical Munsiyari by way of Champawat or those walking their way to Kailash-Mansarovar.

Those who plan a stay in Pithoragarh find themselves plenty to do, be it exploring the temples and towns around or wandering in the wilderness. Thal Kedar, Punyagiri, Rameshwar and Jauljibi in the neighbourhood of Pithoragarh boast an eclectic selection of temples, the venues of annual religious fairs.

Standing sentinel above Pithoragarh are Mts Nanda Devi East, Nanda Devi West, Trishul, Hardeol, Nandakhat, Rajrambha, Bambadhura and the Panchchhuli. Alongside rush the Rivers Ramganga, Gori and Kali offering exciting rapids for river rafting or canoeing, quiet corners for angling and plenty of delightful spots for picnics. Pithoragarh has its share of trekking trails to the glaciers of Milam, Namik, Ralam, Meola and Balati and to Dharchula, Tawaghat, Tijam, Narayan Swami Ashram, Sosa, and Malpa and beyond to Kailash-Mansarovar or Lipu Pass.

Munsiyari, Johar Valley's gateway to the glaciers, is a treasure trove of alpine delights located on the edge of the River Gori Ganga as it threads its way down through forests of oak and pine ablaze with rhododendrons. Around Munsiyari are the alpine lakes of Maheshwari Kund and Thamri Kund and the Munsiyari Bugyal, an alpine meadow full of wildflowers. A quiet place, Munsiyari has tented accommodation as well as Tourist, Forest and PWD Rest Houses.

Udham Singh Nagar

Possibly the most prosperous district in Uttaranchal, Udham Singh Nagar (named in honour of the freedom fighter Udham Singh) is the agricultural and industrial nucleus of the state. Fields of paddy, wheat and sugarcane, and tractors, trolleys and farmhouses apart, there is little to be seen in Udham Singh Nagar. The few places worth visiting include Nanak Matta, a revered pilgrimage for Sikhs and the Nanak Matta Dam on the River Saryu. Nanak Sagar, the reservoir of the dam, has facilities for boating and fishing and is a good place for a layover on the way to or back from Kumaon.

It's a man's world in Kumaon

* Patriarchs rule the roost here.
* Polygamy has divine sanction – polyandry is taboo.
* Males are the superior sex – but women can work in the fields.
* Lower caste women can remarry but not upper caste women –naturally this rule does not extend to the upper caste male.

ADVENTURE SPECIAL

Angling: Mahseer and trout fishing in the River Kosi (Ramnagar), Sharda and Kali (Kumaon); mahseer, goonch and trout in the River Ramganga (Corbett) and for Indian trout at Yamuna Bridge (Mussoorie), Naukuchiya Tal (Nainital), Nanak Sagar (Udham Singh Nagar). Licenses and permits available from the office of the local District Forest Officer.

Mountaineering: *Garhwal* – Mts Kamet (7756 m), Banderpoonch (6316 m), Nanda Devi (7817 m), Chaukhamba (7138 m) etc.

Kumaon – Mts Burphu Dhura (6414 m), Trishuli (7035 m), Tharkot (6100 m), Maiktoli (6800 m), Nanda Khat (6600 m), Sunder Dhunga (6650 m), Panchchhuli Range (I-6350 m, II-6900 m, III-6300 m, IV-6300 m and V-6400 m) Rajrambha (6500 m), Chotta Kailash (6200 m).

For permission, contact:

Indian Mountaineering Foundation, New Delhi,

Nehru Institute of Mountaineering, Uttarkashi.

Paragliding: At Naukuchiya Tal (Nainital) and Mussoorie.

River Rafting: On the Rivers Ganga, Yamuna, Alaknanda, Bhagirathi and Tons in Garhwal and on the Kali Ganga and Sharda in Kumaon. September-November and March-May are the best months for river rafting.

River Ganga: Kaudiyala to Rishikesh – 36 km (12 major rapids).

River Bhagirathi: Matuli to Dunda – 12 km (professional and amateur)

Dharasu to Chham – 12 km ((professional and amateur).

Jangla to Jhala – 20 km (professional and amateur).

Bhaldiana to Tehri – (professional and amateur).

River Yamuna: Barkot to Lakha Mandal – (professional and amateur).

Damta to Yamuna Bridge – (professional and amateur).

River Tons: Mori to Tyuni –32 km (professional and amateur).

River Bhilangna: Ghansali to Gadolia – 32 km (strictly pro!)

River Mandakini: Chandrapuri to Rudraprayag – 30 km (highly pro!)

River Kali Ganga: Jauljibi to Tanakpur – 117 km (professionals only!)

Rock Climbing: *Skiing:* At Auli (Joshimath), Mundali (Chakrata), Dayara Bugyal (Uttarkashi), Munsiyari, Bedni Bugyal (Gwaldam) and Chiplakot (Pithoragarh). Professional coaching facilities and ski equipment is organized by GMVN.

Trekking: The glaciers – Gangotri, Khatling, Milam, Ralam, Tijam, Pindari, Mriguthani, Banderpoonch and Kafni. The places – Har ki Doon, Muni ki Reti, Bedni Bugyal, Nag Tibba, Sunderdhunga, Valley of Flowers, Hemkund Sahib, Madhyamahesh, Tapovan, Namik, Lipu Pass, Roop Kund, Saptrishi Kund, Vasuki Tal, Gaumukh, Kagbhusand Lake and Nachiketa Tal.

Best time to go: April to October except during the monsoons.
Water Sports: Sailing, water skiing, kayaking and canoeing at Asian Barrage, Dak Pathar near Dehradun.
Wildlife Parks: Askot Sanctuary (Pithoragarh), Binsar Sanctuary (Binsar), Nanda Devi National Park, Rajaji National Park, Corbett National Park and Tiger Reserve, Gobind Wildlife Sanctuary (Uttarkashi), Kedarnath Sanctuary and Valley of Flowers.

Eleven Ways to Explore Uttaranchal

Eleven trails, leading to different places and showcasing different aspects of the beautiful state of Uttaranchal. The eleven trails cover the state from end to end – east and west, north and south. First-timers to Uttaranchal can take the trail that ignites the imagination or appeals to the senses – old hands can blaze a new path, head in a different direction or go back to familiar territory.

Trail I: Delhi-Yamunotri

Delhi-Yamunotri via Dehradun (448 km)

Delhi→ 255 km→ Dehradun → 137 km→ Barkot → 43 km→ Hanuman Chatti→ 13 km→ Yamunotri

Delhi-Yamunotri via Chamba (468 km)

Delhi →203 km →Haridwar →40 km →Narendra Nagar →45 km →Chamba →157 km →Hanuman →Chatti → 13 km →Yamunotri

Trail II: Delhi-Gangotri (480 km)

Delhi →203 km → Haridwar → 40 km → Narendra Nagar → 45 km→Chamba→88 km → Uttarkashi →28 km → Bhatwari →52 km → Jangla →16 km → Gangotri

Trail III: Delhi-Kedarnath (490 km)

Delhi → 203 km → Haridwar → 103 km → Devaprayag →100 km → Rudraprayag →40 km→ Khimath → 32 km →Gaurikund → 14 km → Kedarnath (490 km)

Trail IV: Delhi-Badrinath (533 km)

Delhi→203 km→Haridwar→ 138 km→Srinagar→66 km→ Karnaprayag→31 km→Chamoli →51 km→Joshimath→44 km→ Badrinath

Trail V: Delhi-Munsiyari

Delhi-Munsiyari via Haridwar and Bageshwar (665 km)

Delhi→203 km→Haridwar→ 138 km→Srinagar→66 km→ Karnaprayag→70 km→ Gwaldam →46 km→Bageshwar→142 km→ Munsiyari

Delhi-Munsiyari via Kathgodam (567 km)

Delhi→285 km→Kathgodam→ 90 km → Almora →192 km→ Munsiyari

Trail VI: Delhi-Dharchula (630 km)

Delhi→280 km→Haldwani→ 109 km→Tanakpur→75 km→

Champawat→80 km→ Pithoragarh → 87 km→ Dharchula

Trail VII: Delhi-Almora via Nainital & Ranikhet (426 km)

Delhi→285 km→Kathgodam→ 35 km→Nainital→59 km→ Ranikhet→47 km→Almora

Trail VIII: Delhi-Mussoorie-Dhanaulti (314 km)

Delhi→255 km→Dehradun→ 35 km→Mussoorie→24 km→ Dhanaulti

Trail IX: Delhi-Corbett National Park (340 km)

Delhi→163 km→Moradabad→ 97 km→Kashipur→28 km→ Ramnagar→51 km→Dhikala

Trail X: Delhi-Valley of Flowers & Hemkund Sahib (528 km)

Delhi→228 km→Rishikesh→ 180 km→Karnaprayag→82 km→ Joshimath→20 km→Gobindghat →15 km→Ghangaria→3 km→ Valley of Flowers

Trail XI: Char Dham (1825 km)

Delhi→228 km→Rishikesh→ 222 km→Yamunotri→183 km→ Uttarkashi→96 km→Gangotri→ 165 km→Tehri→171 km→ Kedarnath→51 km→Okhimath → 81 km → Chamoli → 51 km → Joshimath→ 44 km→Badrinath→ 330 km→Haridwar→203 km→Delhi

TRAIL I: DELHI-YAMUNOTRI

Attain the high ground in more ways than one with this trail that travels to Yamunotri, sacred shrine and hallowed source of the River Yamuna in the Garhwal Himalayas. In the not-so-distant past, the road to Yamunotri was so unforgiving that few expected to come back and those who ventured forth, undertook it as the grand finale to a devout Hindu life. Happily, that worst case scenario no longer exists and though the road leaves much to be desired, it is good enough for a holiday in the hills.

Not all roads lead to Yamunotri – the two that do travel via Dehradun

TRAIL I: DELHI-YAMUNOTRI

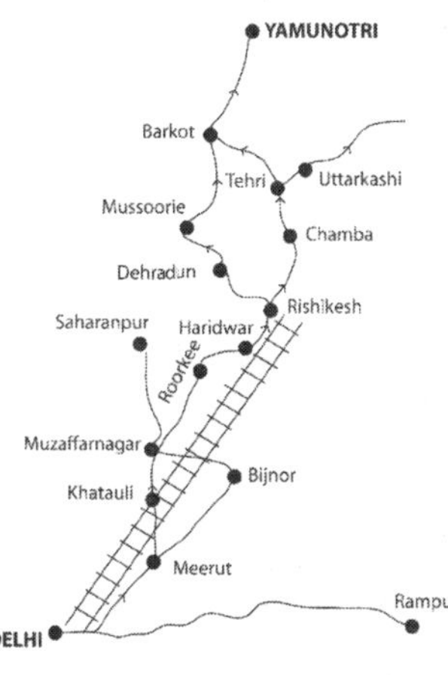

Map not to scale

or Chamba only to catch up with each other at Barkot. Pick either, as there really is not that much to choose between them. Nearly equidistant, both negotiate their way through the grubby small towns of north India before beginning the climb towards the Himalayas, which is when both justify their existence in terms of sheer picturesqueness.

The Routes

Delhi-Yamunotri via Dehradun 433 km

Delhi→240 km→Dehradun→ 137 km→Barkot→43 km→ Hanuman Chatti→13 km→ Yamunotri

Delhi-Yamunotri via Chamba 468 km

Delhi→203 km→Haridwar → 40 km → Narendra Nagar → 45 km → Chamba → 157 km → Hanuman Chatti → 13 km → Yamunotri

Trail Time: 10-12 hours of steady driving at an average speed of 50 km per hour are good enough to get to Hanuman Chatti – road ends on this trail. More realistically, plan on spending the entire day on the road, with judicious breaks for lunch, tea and loo!

Both our trails have only a transitory acquaintance with

Follow the Road

Via Dehradun:
Delhi-Dehradun: 240 km (5-6 hrs)
Dehradun-Barkot: 137 km (4-5 hrs)
Barkot-Hanuman Chatti: 43 km (1.5 hrs)
Hanuman Chatti-Yamunotri: 13 km (1 hr)

Via Chamba:
Delhi-Narendra Nagar: 243 km (5-6 hrs)
Narendra Nagar-Chamba: 45 km (1.5 hrs)
Chamba-Barkot: 115 km (4-5 hrs)
Barkot-Hanuman Chatti: 43 km (1.5 hrs)
Hanuman Chatti-Yamunotri: 13 km (1 hr)

Timely Getaway

Rise and shine at the crack of dawn, even if you think early mornings are only for the birds. While the poor worm may not benefit from the 'early to rise' adage, early morning motorists are the lucky breed who get away before Delhi's terrifying traffic gets going.
Alternate travel options include a flight to Jolly Grant, the nearest airport outside Dehradun, trains to either Dehradun or Rishikesh and/or a bus to Yamunotri. Also available in season, are a goodly number of coach tours between Delhi and Yamunotri.

National Highway 24 till Ghaziabad, less than 20 km out of Delhi. Then onwards, the trail travels along State Highway 45, great in some sections, good in others and absolutely ghastly in certain places. Still, the stretch to Dehradun is a popular one with motorists who still find it more convenient than the non-stop Shatabdi Express to Doon.

Stopovers

Fast forward past Ghaziabad, Meerut, Muzaffarnagar, Roorkee or Saharanpur to Haridwar, the portal that gets you to Hari (God Vishnu). Not that these places don't have something or the other going for them, they do, but the trail is in a hurry to get to the hills.

Haridwar & Rishikesh (340 m): The holy towns on the banks of the River Ganga have figured on pilgrim itineraries from the beginning of Hinduism. Consecrated by the Hindu Trinity of Brahma, Vishnu and Mahesh, venerated as a Shaktipeeth and hallowed by the waters of the Ganga, Haridwar and Rishikesh promise Hindus instant moksha and ultimate nirvana. The only constants in Rishikesh and Haridwar are its holy cows – ashrams, gurukuls, temples, ghats, priests, pilgrims and peripatetic mendicants, all others are transitory! Those who stop by, do so only long enough to take a holy dip, sluice off a few sins before moving on to the next stage, of life or the road as the case maybe.

Dehradun (640 m): The next stop on our trail is Dehradun, erstwhile retreat of the retired, now happening as the interim capital of Uttaranchal.

First Stop for Food, Fuel, Fowl & Flowers

The Chital Grand on the road to Dehradun is not exactly the kind of serai Sher Shah Suri had in mind for tired travellers when he built the Grand Trunk Road but does very well by 21st century's travellers. It provides hot pakoras to go with hot chai and clean loos in a salubrious setting of gardens filled with flowers and birds.

A new pride of government administrators lays down new laws from buildings built more than a century ago when the most exciting event in Doon was the arrival or departure of troops quartered in the Cantonment. (Dera = Camp + Dun=Valley adds up to Dehradun, the camp in the valley.) The wear and tear down the years has eroded much of Doon's magic reducing it to another hot and dusty, grime encrusted north Indian town crowded with hotels and shops and packed with people. With one exception – the cool and clean looking green hills that beckon from the not-so-distant horizon.

Mussoorie (2005 m): Who but an Englishman would establish a town in the hills for no reason other than to escape the heat of the plains? Discovered, in a manner of speaking, by a Captain Young in 1826, Mussoorie boomed as a cool getaway. Homes proliferated, schools flourished and hotels mushroomed in its pretty setting aided and abetted by both climate and proximity to Delhi. Till honeymooners hit upon Mussoorie, it remained a quiet summer retreat for the elite and princes of industry, who built holiday homes for their families. Nowadays, Mussoorie is more the domain of tired travellers and jaded hoteliers than of India's rich and famous. But there is another Mussoorie, hidden well away from those that crowd the Mall and haunt Kulri Bazaar, the Mussoorie of Landour, Hathipani, Sisters' Bazaar, Camel's Back and Happy Valley.

Chamba (1524 m): The drive to Chamba is an unusually pleasant one, considering the fact that the heights are yet to be scaled. Sparkling like silver in the sunlight, the River Henval plays hide and seek till Nagni, the little village where the road begins its ascent towards Chamba.

Now Chamba, that's a secret never to be shared. Untouched, undiscovered and as yet unscathed by developmental activity, this little town in Tehri offers breathtaking views of the Himalayas on the one side

Tehri Dam – Damned or Doomed?

The 260.5 m high rock fill Tehri dam, located in a seismically active zone on the edge of the central Himalayan seismic gap, close to the epicentre of the devastating Uttarkashi earthquake of 1991, has been controversial from its inception. The pro-dam lobby believes it will transform the lives of the people of Garhwal. Anti-dam lobbyists say sure! One quake measuring 8 on the Richter Scale and, within the hour, Rishikesh will be under 260 m of water, Haridwar will be totally submerged to be soon followed by Bijnor, Meerut, Hapur and Bulandshahar.

countered by equally impressive views of the river valley on the other side. Unassuming little hotels and a Forest Rest House provide ample accommodation for those in the know. Those who aren't (in the know) drive 11 km to New Tehri, the ultra modern township that has sprung up to rehabilitate those displaced by the Tehri Dam.

Barkot (1280 m): Its either river rafters or pilgrims who know Barkot. For others, Barkot is another little hamlet of precipitous houses packed tight around a narrow road made even harder to negotiate by jaywalking residents, snoozing cows and kids at play.

Hanuman Chatti (2400 m): The end of the road, literally and metaphorically. This grimy little hill town is the hotspot for hundreds of pilgrims heading for Yamunotri. Hanuman Chatti thrives on pilgrims and abounds with dharamshalas, rest houses, lodges and small hotels offering the barest minimum in comforts – lest you forget this is a pilgrimage.

Yamunotri (3185 m): It takes a killer of a climb – 5 to 6 hours, 13 km and uphill all the way along a narrow track to get to Yamunotri, birthplace of the sacred River Yamuna. Luckily there are ponies and palanquins for the old, the infirm and the idle. Costs vary between Rs 500 and Rs 1500 respectively. Crude though they are, the dandis or palanquins are pretty comfortable and hence cost more. For a really cheap, albeit uncomfortable ride, travel piggyback for Rs 300. Halfway up is the small town of Janki Chatti, cleaner and so infinitely more inviting than Hanuman Chatti. Yamunotri and Janki Chatti both have enough accommodation for pilgrims – a bed, a bath and a place to park your worldly possessions.

Yamunotri stands on the western flank of the Bandarpoonch Mountain (6315 m) and is almost always inundated. Either by snow or by visitors – open only for a short season between May and October, Yamunotri receives a steady stream of 2000 plus pilgrims a day, not counting trekkers and tourists. Most visitors are satisfied after visiting the Yamunotri Temple dedicated to the Goddess Yamuna, the hot spring at Surya Kund (rice and potatoes cook in a trice in its blistering waters), Yamuna Bai Kund and the Divya Shila. The resolute travel further to Sapta Rishi Kund, the true source of the River Yamuna, a gruelling 16-hour climb over ice and rock to be undertaken strictly in the company of guides.

Homeward Bound

You can either retrace the track on the return journey or can opt for the alternate route for variety. So if the road to Yamunotri went by way of Dehradun, Mussoorie and Barkot, the descent to Delhi can be via Chamba and Rishikesh.

Legend & Lore

River Yamuna – daughter of Surya, the Sun God and sister of Yama, the God of Death, born in a glacial lake high in the Garhwal Himalayas – surges down from its mountain abode and journeys across the plains of north India to become one with the Rivers Ganga and Saraswati at Prayag, Allahabad.

After their blissful sangam, Saraswati, always subterranean, remains elusive as ever, Ganga flows on to merge with the ocean at Ganga Sagar but Yamuna vanishes off the face of the earth. Legend tells us that Yamuna, beloved of Krishna, metamorphoses into a cloud of stream to unite with the Supreme One.

The devout believe that a dip in the waters of the Yamuna is equivalent to seven in the sacred Ganga. Why? Because sibling solidarity has the power to ease the fear of death and better still, guarantee a painless passing.

ASIDES: SIDE BY SIDE

Chakrata (2135 m, 92 km from Dehradun): Home of the exotic looking Jaunsari tribe, this pretty hill station is popular for its serenity.

Dhanaulti (2250 m, 25 km from Mussoorie): Tranquil retreat tucked in the middle of forests, perfect for an interlude. Hotels, Luxury Campsite, GMVN Tourist Bungalow and Forest Rest House provide accommodation.

Kempty Falls (1524 m, 15 km from Mussoorie): The biggest and the best waterfall offering fun, frolic and fab views of the valley below.

Lakha Mandal (1090 m): 6 km to the left of Kuwa (60 km), on the Mussoorie-Yamunotri road, marks the spot where the Kauravas commissioned a palace of lacquer for their Pandava brethren. Not because they loved them but because they were desperate to polish them off!

Mundali (129 km from Dehradun): Great ski slopes and panoramic views – Alas! Only accessible via a dirt track from Chakrata (36 km) suitable for off-road vehicles. A Forest Rest House is the only accommodation available at Mundali.

New Tehri (1600 m, 11 km from Chamba): Modern township housing those displaced by the Tehri Dam, with a full complement of hotels and rest houses, small restaurants and shops.

Rajaji National Park: Three sanctuaries – Chilla, Motichur and Rajaji – combine to make up this park in the Shivalik Hills. Mixed deciduous and semi-deciduous forests house elephants, hyenas, tigers, muntjac, deer, goral, neelgai, wild boar, monkeys and many species of birds.

Sahastradhara: Waterfall and sulphur springs close to Mussoorie. Stay over at PWD Rest House.
Tehri (770 m, 22 km from Chamba): Headquarters of the district of Tehri, currently notorious as the site of the controversial Tehri Dam.
Yamuna Bridge (30 km from Mussoorie): Anglers stake out a spot but with a permit from Divisional Forest Officer, 5 Tilak Road, Dehradun. (Tel:0135-223794).

TRAIL II: DELHI-GANGOTRI

Hail Mother Ganges! River of India, cradle of civilization, giver of life and symbol of redemption, dearly beloved and relentlessly polluted, she begins her journey where our trail ends, 3050 m up in the Himalayas. Her 2525 km voyage begins at Gangotri, swooping and sweeping her way across the Indo-Gangetic Plain to merge with the ocean at Ganga Sagar Island in the Bay of Bengal.

As the river descends, chaffing and straining to get free of restrictions imposed by the dense forests and high mountains, it creates an incomparably beautiful river valley. The trail takes the same path as the river, except to go the opposite way, to finish where it all began.

The Route: (480 km)

Delhi→203 km→Haridwar→ 40 km→Narendra Nagar→45 km →Chamba→88 km→Uttarkashi → 28 km→ Bhatwari → 52 km → Jangla → 16 km → Gangotri

TRAIL II : DELHI-GANGOTRI

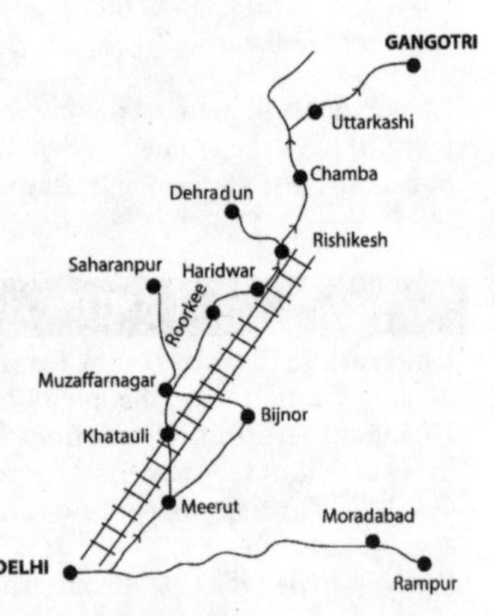

* Map not to scale

Follow the Road

Delhi-Haridwar: 203 km (4 hrs)
Haridwar-Narendra Nagar: 40 km (1 hr)
Narendra Nagar-Chamba: 45 km (1.5 hrs)
Chamba-Uttarkashi: 88 km (3.5 hrs)
Uttarkashi-Bhatwari: 28 km (1 hr)
Bhatwari-Jangla: 52 km (2 hrs)
Jangla-Gangotri: 16 km (.5 hr)

Trail Time: 13-14 hours of driving time, worked out on the assumption that the average driving speed would be around 50 kmph in the plains and 30 kmph in the mountains. The given time doesn't take into account the possibility of frequent halts for lunch, loo or chai or stops for photo-ops and scenic views.

Stopovers

Haridwar (202m): When the gods decided to dwell in the Himalayas, they chose Haridwar as their doorway, a reality reinforced by countless Hindus who begin their teertha-yatras at Haridwar. This ancient city is on the itinerary of every fervent Hindu, and alive or dead, they all make it here. Non-Hindus come as well, as did Huien Tsang, traveller extraordinaire of I Millennium CE, the Beatles, Kate Winslet and Goldie Hawn and countless others drawn by Haridwar's promise of moksha and nirvana.

Haridwar is a city of ashrams, temples and bathing ghats crowded with pilgrims and pujaris. Its most permanent residents are sanyasis, sadhus and swamis. Haridwar should rate more than a mention in despatches, so do stop and take a holy dip, trace your ancestry or shoot a few pictures and, if nothing else, eat a pure vegetarian meal at one of its numerous 'hotels'.

Narendra Nagar (1175 m): Barely 15 km out of Rishikesh and the Rishikesh-Chamba road stops at Narendra Nagar. This capital of the kingdom of Tehri was built in 1895 by the then Maharaja of Tehri, Narendra Singh, who translocated his capital to this more scenic locale in the Shivalik foothills. The Maharaja's efforts to create a capital city befitting his stature can be seen in the fine buildings and clever town planning.

Thick jungle tracts, cooler ambience and a higher altitude were just some ways in which the new site scored over Tehri. Actually, the area has a long and venerable past dating back to Vedic period when sages and sadhus meditated and practised severe penance to please the gods.

Though few people stop at Narendra Nagar in their hurry to get on with it, there are those who

Quick Getaway

Give yourself a break Bearing in mind that the drive ahead is a long haul of 13-14 hours, jump the gun to beat the traffic, catch the greens and miss the reds. This involves organization on a war footing – pack those bags, batten the house down, get to bed on time and WAKE UP when the alarm goes!

Alternate travel options: Flights to Dehradun's Jolly Grant Airport/train to Haridwar and/or bus from Narendra Nagar to Gangotri. In season, coach tours are available between Delhi and Gangotri.

make the trip specially to stay at Ananda Spa Resort, India's first destination spa resort. Because there is nothing so therapeutic as wholesome food, exercise and plenty of clean, fresh air. And if the therapy happens in a maharaja's palace, as it does at Ananda, better still.

Chamba (1524 m): The road, climbing, winding its way up to Gangotri, takes a breather at Chamba, a small town with grandstand views. The Himalayas dominate the landscape, presenting a cool contrast to the heat haze rising from the valley below where the river gleams like a silver thread snaking its way alongside the metallic grey of the road. That's the one that has travelled to Chamba and will negotiate its way to Gangotri via the district headquarters at Uttarkashi.

Uttarkashi (1158 m): Uttar + Kashi = Northern Kashi, ergo the abode of Shiva in the north and thus deemed by devout Hindus to have the same merit as Varanasi.

Encircled by the holy Rivers Bhagirathi, Varuna and Asi, Uttarkashi takes its spiritual eminence seriously. It once had 365 temples, one for each day of the year. Luckily for tourists, the temples have been reduced to manageable numbers, the important ones being dedicated to Shiva, Kali, Parsurama, Dattatreya, Bhairon and Annapurna Devi.

In its other avatar, Uttarkashi is the adventure capital of Uttaranchal imparting professional training in mountaineering and adventure sports at the renowned Nehru Institute of Mountaineering. The region around Uttarkashi is ideal terrain for treks, rock climbing and mountaineering. Accommodation is available, albeit limited in quality and quantity. Small cafés and dhabas serve mainly vegetarian food; non-vegetarian cuisine and alcohol are available and allowed but not encouraged.

Bhatwari (1218 m): Fast forward unless you are a ski dude, in which case, slalom to the left. Possibly the best ski runs in all of Uttaranchal are to be found at Dayarabugyal,

Folklore or Forests?

Legend tells us that Shiva contained the powerful flow of the Ganga in his matted locks – otherwise she would have swept away all that came in her way.

In more tangible terms, it is the dense birch, oak, pine and deodar forests growing on the slopes of the Bhagirathi that contain the might of the river. In a country where the battle to conserve/preserve existing forests has all but been lost to the growing pressure of population, these forest slopes come as a pleasant surprise.

barely 16 km from Bhatwari. Insider's tip for skiers – stay at Bhatwari and ski at Dayara.

Jangla (2575 m): Jangla figures on the trail for two reasons. One, it has accommodation and who wants to be out in the cold! Second, the 20 km stretch between Jangla and Jhala presents superlative white water rafting – for amateurs as well as professionals. Just about beginning its descent, the Bhagirathi is in full spate in this stretch. Wild, wilful, white, frothing and foaming, the fast flowing waters of the Bhagirathi spill over rocks and eddy around corners in their eagerness to reach the plains.

Gangotri (3048 m): A temple built by Amar Singh Thapa in the 18th century, later restored by the Maharani of Jaipur, commemorates the place the Ganga is believed to have made her descent. A stone close to the temple marks the spot where King Bhagirath sat in his long-term penance to please Shiva. So sacred is Gangotri that the Pandavas came here to atone for the fratricide committed by them during the mega battle in the Hindu epic, Mahabharata. Close to the temple is the Jalmagna Shivaling, a natural stone Shivaling hidden by the waters of the Bhagirathi that only makes its public appearance in early winter.

To those of you thinking, 'Is that it?' we say hang on! There's more on offer here than spiritual nirvana especially where the Bhagirathi emerges from its temple hideaway to surge into the Bhairon Ghati gorge through the Gaurikund, by way of a series of cascades that create an incredible sound and light show.

Gaumukh (3892 m): The spiritual, metaphysical and material lifeline of India's billions makes a dramatic entrance at Gaumukh, a huge cavern that long lay hidden beneath the gargantuan Gangotri glacier. When global warming and cosmic meltdown forced the glacier to recede, it became evident that the river actually began its earthly sojourn not at Gangotri but 15 km ahead at Gaumukh. The road to Gaumukh is neither hazardous nor the one-way ticket it used to be, though the waters are icy enough to freeze the blood and the air cold enough to turn it blue. Luckily, there are many little shops and stalls at Chirwasa and Bhojwasa that serve lifesaving hot tea (alas, no brandy!) as well as PWD and Forest Rest Houses at Bhojwasa and Gangotri to thaw out.

What's in a Name?

The River Ganga dons many a guise and masquerades under many a name. For starters, try Bhagirathi, Mandakini, Alaknanda, Jahnavi, Dhauli Ganga, Pindar Ganga, Nandakini or Hooghly! At its font, the Ganga goes by the name of Bhagirathi, honouring the man whose years and years of penance constrained the Goddess Ganga to leave her celestial abode and descend to earth.

Return Journey

With the future assured and a measure of moksha attained, it's time to return home. This time round, go with the flow. Follow the river on its downward journey till Tehri. Then letting the river go its way, the trail returns to Rishikesh, Haridwar/via Narendra Nagar and Chamba. Delhi and journey's end is only a few hours away.

ASIDES: SIDE BY SIDE

Ananda Spa (39 km from Rishikesh): Detoxification, oil massages, yoga, ayurveda, aromatherapy, organic food and exercise at India's first destination spa and resort in what once alternated as the Maharaja of Tehri's summer palace and viceregal retreat on the banks of the River Ganga. (Tel: 1378-227500 Fax: 1378-227550/011-27948870, 27947265, Fax: 011-25708542).

Dayarabugyal (3048 m, 16 km from Bhatwari): A sprawling alpine meadow famed for its natural beauty, breathtaking views of the Himalayas and – hold your breath – ski slopes spread over 28 km. For accommodation, try village huts at Dyara or settle for accommodation in Bhatwari.

Dodi Tal (3007 m): Anglers' delight! Just 30 km (only on foot) from Dyarabugyal you get to a sparkling blue alpine lake densely populated with Himalayan trout. Forest Rest House, log cabin and campsite available but first get a license from DFO, Uttarkashi.

Harsil (2745 m, 40 km from Bhatwari): The epitome of an alpine village – sylvan setting, apple orchards, pretty belles et al. Also has PWD and Forest Rest Houses for those keen on staying over.

Kedar Tal (4500 m, 18 km from Gangotri): A rough track takes the intrepid traveller to this beautiful lake lying in the shadow of Thalaiyasagar peak.

Sat Tal (2987 m, 8 km from Jangla): Seven pretty lakes showcase the Himalayas to perfection but hurry – two have already dried up!

Tapovan (4460 m, 4 km from Gaumukh): A steep climb to the base of the Shivaling Peak to see an alpine meadow strewn with wildflowers in summer.

Nandanvan (6510 m): On the trekking route across the Gangotri Glacier to Vasuki Tal and Badrinath. No accommodation or refreshment facilities but still worth the effort.

Alpine Lakes: Nachiketa Tal, Khara Tal, Arwa Tal and Vasuki Tal.

Geysers: Thermal springs at Garampani (6 km from Uttarkashi) and Gangani (12 km from Bhatwari).

Maneri (1298 m, 14 km from Uttarkashi): Dam across the Bhagirathi curbs its swift flowing waters to create a pretty picnic spot. Have lunch here.

TRAIL III: DELHI - KEDARNATH

The holiest of the holies! Sanctified and scenic! Standing at the source of the graceful Mandakini, in close proximity to the snow-encased Kedarnath Peak (6970 m), the Hindu shrine of Kedarnath is highly revered as one of 12 Jyotirlingas where Shiva, Protector and Destroyer, Lord of the Mountains, manifests himself as Divine Light. Fortunately for travellers of a non-saffron hue, the shrine and its setting both live up to the hype.

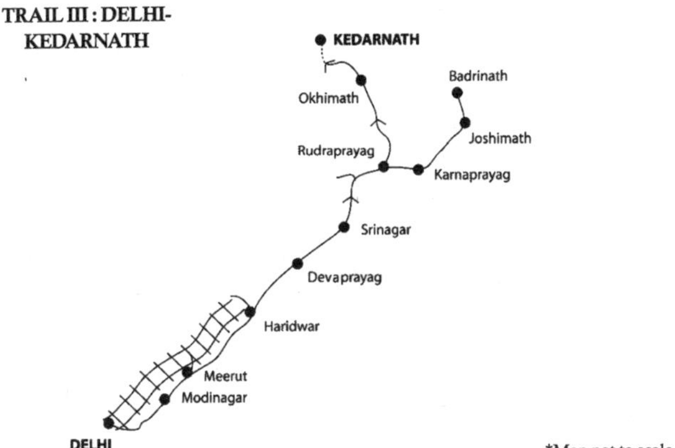

The Route: 490 km

Delhi→203 km→Haridwar→ 103 km→Devaprayag→100 km→ Rudraprayag→40 km→Okhimath →32 km→Gaurikund→14 km→ Kedarnath

Trail Time: Anywhere between 14 hrs and two days.

As part of the Char Dham Yatra, the journey to Kedarnath is over and done with in one day but as ours is more vacation than voyage of contrition, we can do it at leisure.

Follow the Road
Delhi-Haridwar: 203 km (4 hrs)
Haridwar-Devaprayag: 103 km (1 hr)
Devaprayag-Rudraprayag: 100 km (1.5 hrs)
Rudraprayag-Okhimath: 40 km (3.5 hrs)
Okhimath-Gaurikund: 32 km (1 hr)
Gaurikund-Kedarnath: 14 km (2 hrs)

The first stage of the journey brings us to Haridwar, barely 4-5 hours out of Delhi and good for a stop, especially if the departure from Delhi is delayed. So stay overnight at or in the vicinity of Haridwar, take a holy dip and earn a few brownie points with the gods.

Quick Getaway

What beats sleeping late on vacation? Scoring one over Delhi's interminable traffic. And since the only time one can actually achieve the impossible is on holiday, let's do it! Rise and shine with the sun, hit the road bright and early and by the time the first bus catches up, you're home and dry in Kedarnath.

Other ways to do it: Fly to Dehradun's Jolly Grant Airport/ take a train to Haridwar and catch a cab or bus to Kedarnath. Roadways and private bus owners operate daily coach tours to Kedarnath in peak season.

Stopovers

Haridwar (202 m): Welcome to Haridwar – first port of call on the road to Uttaranchal and last stop on the way to heaven. Haridwar, where Hindus congregate to pay their respects to the river they call Ganga Maiya, confident in their belief that the sacred waters of the holy Ganga have the powers to wash away all sins. This much revered holy city on the banks of the River Ganga was further sanctified by a fall out of divine nectar during the churning of the oceans.

Haridwar receives thousands of visitors but the one who left his mark was none other than Vishnu, Preserver, Protector and member of the Hindu Trinity. The most important site in Haridwar, also the one most visited, is Har ki Pauri, where the Lord left the imprints of his feet. One of the most spiritually satisfying sights in Haridwar is the early morning/evening aarti at the bathing ghat besides Har Ki Pauri. Hundreds of lit diyas are placed on the River Ganga amidst the chanting of hymns and the chimes of temple bells.

Haridwar is well equipped to deal with the recurrent deluge of visitors – ashrams, dharamshalas, hotels and now even resorts along the banks of the Ganga offer accommodation. Haridwar is an appealing stopover, especially for those looking for answers to cosmic conundrums.

And if the sundry charms of Hinduism's seventh holiest city don't appeal, then move along the Ganga to Rishikesh (22 km). If Rishikesh was good enough for Ringo Starr and company, it's certainly good enough for us. An important centre for yoga and meditation, Rishikesh abounds in gurukuls, ashrams and yogashalas. A few kilometres ahead of

Rishikesh, connecting the two banks of the Ganga, is the famous Laxmana Jhoola, once a rickety contraption of sticks and ropes, now reinforced with steel cables. Muni ki Reti on the road to Kedarnath offers excellent training facilities for trekking, rock climbing, mountaineering and river rafting aided and abetted by the Garhwal Mandal Vikas Nigam. Tourist Bungalows and ashrams provide reasonable accommodation at extremely affordable prices.

Thirty kilometres from Rishikesh, the road which has been faithfully edging closer to the Ganga reaches Byasi, a small town with nothing to warrant this mention except that the road now begins its ascent towards Devaprayag.

Devaprayag (813 m): Confluence of two mighty mountain rivers, the Bhagirathi and Alaknanda, whose pooled resources are hereafter known as the Ganga. And in India, any place where rivers meet is a sacred site, venerated and visited by the devout, so too with Devaprayag. Adi Shankaracharya, the 9th century Hindu mystic, saint, philosopher and teacher, established a temple dedicated to Lord Rama at Devaprayag. There are, of course, many other temples in Devaprayag enshrining different Hindu deities like Hanuman, Shiva, Badrinath and Kala Bhairava.

Conveniently placed to muster energies for the pilgrimage to Kedarnath and Badrinath, Devaprayag has adequate hotel accommodation and a PWD Rest House too.

Rudraprayag (610 m): Two hundred Shiva shrines, the muddy union of the Rivers Mandakini and Alaknanda, site of Narada Muni's penance and the place where Shiva materialized as Rudra – small wonder that Rudraprayag is a popular destination. The mid-sized township spreads around the gorge created by two powerful rivers, eddying and swirling as if locked in mortal combat. It also happens to be smack bang in the path of the slipstream of pilgrims heading for Kedarnath and Badrinath. So cashing in on this annual exodus, Rudraprayag caters to them with hotels and hostelries, dhabas and shops.

Okhimath (1311 m): The winter residence of Lord Kedarnath, set against a backdrop of towering mountains and tall peaks that make up the Kedarnath Range, is justifiably famous for its hot springs that are believed to have therapeutic powers. The Lord of the Mountains stays in Okhimath till the Kedarnath shrine reopens in May, when he ceremonially returns to his real home. Apart from the pilgrims visiting the Shiva and Parvati Temple, Okhimath is on the itinerary of acutely addicted trekking junkies, who stop here for provision, ponies and pointsmen.

Gaurikund (1981m): A 32 km long ascent towards the serried ranks of Himalayan mountains with the Mandakini flowing alongside the road is what it takes to arrive at Gaurikund, where Gauri (Parvati) prayed to become the consort of Shiva. She did and the site got sanctified.

The road ends here. So say goodbye to cabs and cars at Gaurikund and start walking. On the return journey, stop at Gaurikund's sulphur springs, which despite the steam and smell are the perfect cure for those aching limbs and weary bodies. Reasonable accommodation is available at PWD Rest Houses and hotels.

Legend & Lore

Having disposed of one hundred of their Kaurava cousins, the Pandavas felt the need to repent. Hoping that Shiva would oblige, the Pandavas went off to look for him in the Garhwal Himalayas but Shiva turned himself into a bull and got away. When the Pandavas caught up with him, Shiva disappeared into the ground leaving only his hump behind. That one can be seen and worshipped at Kedarnath. Other parts of Shiva's anatomy surfaced at four more places, like his face at Rudranath, arms at Tungnath, belly at Madhyamaheshwar and the famous dreadlocks at Kalpeshwar, making a grand total of five Shivas or Panch Kedars.

An interesting footnote to this unusual story is provided by the prediction that another Kedar, the Bhawishya Kedar, will appear when Kedarnath disappears after a cataclysmic event that would change the topography of the region. No prizes for guessing what the earth-shattering occurrence could be.

Kedarnath (3594 m): Limber up, shake a leg and hope like crazy that those aerobic classes work. It takes a sharp, steep climb of 14 km to reach Kedarnath, but luckily the ascent is as picturesque as it is tough. For the first 7 km, the bridle path sheers 600 m up the hill along the Mandakini, through deep green woods, past mountain streams and cascades to arrive at Rambara (2591 m).

Rambara is a good place to break journey, grab a plateful of parathas, cups of tea and fuel up for the walk ahead. Thankfully, the pathway evens out to make for an easier second half.

The temple at Kedarnath is an impressive one and deeply satisfying for those who have huffed and puffed all the way up. One thousand years old and built by Adi Shankaracharya in the 9th century, the shrine at Kedarnath stands on a plateau, its slate grey structure silhouetted against a perfect backdrop of lofty peaks and rugged mountains. Outside the temple, guarding the entrance as it were, sits Shiva's faithful companion Nandi, while enshrined within is a conical rock formation (the hump), representing Shiva as Sadashiva. The temple walls are decorated with friezes and sculptures of Hindu deities. Close by are the ruins of a temple dating back to the Pandavas while behind the temple is the samadhi of Adi Shankaracharya himself.

Beyond Kedarnath lie multiple levels of mountain ranges that include such stalwarts as Mt Kamet, Nanda Devi, Kedarnath, Vasuki and Choukhamba and in between are exquisitely beautiful bugyals, the high altitude alpine meadows of Garhwal. The entire region offers the ultimate in trekking, mountaineering and camping.

Homeward Ho

A right turn and another haul of 495 km bring the trail back to Delhi. The easiest way to return home is to revise the onward journey – the one big advantage being one's been there and done that. Those who want something new albeit long, take the road to Karnaprayag (20 km from Rudraprayag), Gwaldam (65 km), Kausani (40 km), Ranikhet (62 km), Ramnagar (95 km) and Moradabad (90 km) back to Delhi (158 km). That adds up to a grand total of 936 km but makes up because enroute stopovers could include the charming Kumaon resorts of Gwaldam, Kausani and Ranikhet as well as the amazing Corbett National Park.

ASIDES: SIDE BY SIDE

Chorabari Tal (2 km from Kedarnath): The source of the Mandakini lies in the crystal clear waters of this glacial lake close to the main shrine of Kedarnath.

Chopta (2700 m, 37 km from Okhimath): Rest Houses and hotels on the road to Gopeshwar at what is billed as the prettiest place in Garhwal, in the midst of bugyals and mountains.

Kedarnath Sanctuary: High in the Himalayas lies this 967sq km wildlife sanctuary and park housing rare Himalayan flora and fauna. Best time for a visit is between April and June and September to November. Accommodation is available at the Forest huts courtesy of DFO, Kedarnath Forest Division, Gopeshwar.

Madhyamaheshwar (3490 m, 30 km from Okhimath): Hot springs sprout where Shiva's stomach surfaced (see Legend & Lore for more info).

ASIDES: SIDE BY SIDE

Rudranath (2286 m, 54 km from Chopta): Another of the Panch Kedars – the face of Shiva appeared here.
Syalsaur (1920 m, 25 km from Rudraprayag): GMVN Tourist Village and holiday resort on the banks of the Mandakini.
Sonprayag (1829 m, 5 km from Gaurikund): Take a dip at the confluence of the Mandakini and Vasuki Rivers to reserve a seat in heaven.
Srinagar (579 m, 34 km from Rudraprayag): Not the capital of Kashmir, but hopeful of becoming the capital of Uttaranchal.
Trijugi Narayan (1982 m, 17 km from Gaurikund): The sacred fire still burns in the temple where the marriage of Shiva and Parvati was solemnized.
Tungnath (3680 m, 4 km from Chopta): A tough walk up a steep gradient gets to Tungnath Temple at the foot of Chandrashila Peak (4090 m). One of the Panch Kedars because Shiva's arm landed here.
Vasuki Lake (4315 m, 6 km from Kedarnath): High altitude lake ringed by green meadows perfectly showcased against the impressive Kedarnath Range.

TRAIL IV: DELHI-BADRINATH

'There are many sacred spots of pilgrimage in the heavens, earth and the nether world, but there has been none equal to Badri, nor shall there be.'

Much in the same manner as a devout Hindu's existence is incomplete without paying obeisance to the Lord Badrinath, a sojourn in the Himalayan heights of Garhwal remains half done without a visit to this beautiful valley of the Nar and Narayan ranges. The best part of a journey to Badrinath is the getting there bit. In the plains, the road meanders its way into the picture of rustic tranquility – sparkling streams, clusters of villages, herds of cattle, fields of young wheat, tender green paddy or golden flowering mustard, depending on the season.

But once in the hills, rustic charms give way before a bone- jarring and spine-chilling ride. Lofty mountains and the fast flowing Alaknanda flank the not-so-well-sprung road up to Badrinath. Blind corners, sharp curves, hairpin bends, suspension bridges, steep gradients and deep chasms contribute their bit to the breathtaking ride and if you are very, very fortunate, then a landfall or two might generate some more excitement.

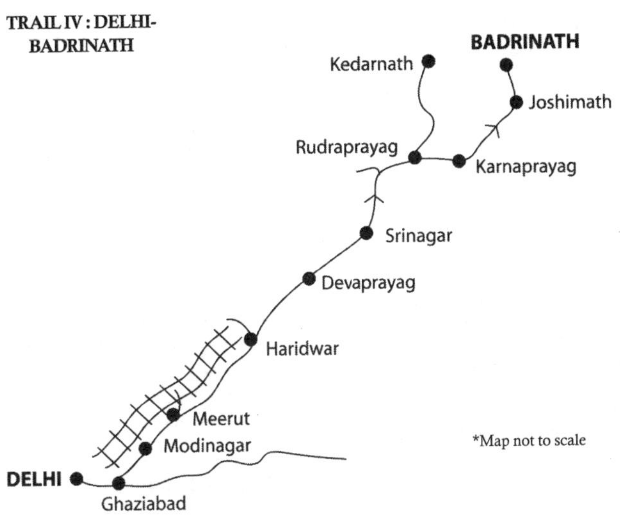

The Route: 533 km

Delhi→225 km→Rishikesh→ 115 km→Srinagar→66 km→ Karnaprayag→31 km→Chamoli → 51 km→Joshimath→44 km→ Badrinath

Trail Time: Take a day, take two or take three! This is a trail designed for holidaymakers heading for the hills, not pilgrims atoning for sins (past, present and future ones) and in a hurry to get it over and done with.

Technically, the trail to Badrinath entails 13 hours of driving at speeds that vary between 50 kmph on the plains and 40 kmph on mountain roads.

Follow the Road

Delhi-Rishikesh: 225 km (5 hrs)
Rishikesh-Srinagar: 115 km (3 hrs)
Srinagar-Karnaprayag: 66 km (2 hrs)
Karnaprayag-Chamoli: 31 km (1 hr)
Chamoli-Joshimath: 51 km (1.5 hrs)
Joshimath-Vishnuprayag: 12 km (1.5 hrs)
Vishnuprayag-Badrinath: 32 km (1 hr)

Stopovers

Rishikesh (340 m): Ensconced by rolling hills on three sides and

Exit Delhi

Exit Delhi as early and as fast as you can. In case you are tempted to lie abed, spare a thought for the climb up 3000 m on a curvaceous mountain road with no streetlights and little help in sight.

Other ways to Badrinath

Flight to Dehradun's Jolly Grant Airport/train to Haridwar or Rishikesh and then by road to Badrinath. Cabs, rental cars, roadways buses and coach tours are easily available, especially in season.

roiling waters of the Ganga on the fourth, Rishikesh has the perfect ambience to indulge in a bit of soul searching or give in to the urge for action. Ashrams dot the riverside, offering a retreat for those looking for spiritual sustenance or quiet introspection. Gurukuls conduct classes in Hindu philosophy, meditation, yoga, Ayurveda and naturopathy using the traditional, time honoured teaching style that is as old as time.

Hotels, GMVN Tourist Bungalow, cottages, resorts and campsites set a little way out of town cater to the swashbuckling traveller looking to achieve physical nirvana. And they find it in the turbulent waters of the River Ganga as it slaloms rapidly downhill from its high altitude home in the Himalayas, only to skid to a more sedate pace at Rishikesh. The abrupt deceleration in momentum creates demanding white water rapids and torrents to gladden the hearts of river runners and rafters.

Srinagar (579 m): A capital city in the mountains but not in the same league as the capital of Jammu & Kashmir. Nevertheless, Uttaranchal's Srinagar, built along the left bank of the Alaknanda, was the seat of the powerful kingdom of Garhwal for 300 long years and aspires to be capital of the new state of Uttaranchal some day soon.

Legend & Lore

Childless couples are blessed with progeny if they can gratify Shiva at the Kamleshwar Mahadev Temple. To do this, they have to stay up on the night of Vaikunth Chaturdashi (November) and ensure their ghee lamps don't die out. And then if the Lord wills, they shall multiply! Not bad for one night's loss of sleep.

In common with other places in Kumaon and Garhwal, Srinagar has its quota of temples. The Raj Rajeshwari, Dhari Devi, Kesho Rai Math, Shankar Math, Guru Gorakhnath and Kamleshwar Mahadev temples are some of the big ones in and around Srinagar. Srinagar is a big town, big in comparison to the average size of towns in Uttaranchal and has a modest number of hotels and lodges for those interested in staying over.

Karnaprayag (832 m): One of the Panch Prayags in Uttaranchal, hallowed and honoured because they commemorate the confluence of Hinduism's holiest rivers. It all began with the River Ganga's forceful descent to earth threatening to wash away all that came in her way. Shiva was called upon to contain the torrent and he did so by trapping it in his coiled locks. Shiva released the Ganga in small manageable streams that go by the names of Alaknanda, Bhagirathi, Mandakini, Pindar and Dhauli Ganga. Their five confluences at the Panch Prayags are mandatory stopovers for Hindus in search of salvation.

The Alaknanda meets the Pindar at Karnaprayag, a small town named for the munificent Karan of the Mahabharata fame. Aside from the confluence, two ancient temples dedicated to Uma (Parvati) and Karan are the tourist attractions in Karnaprayag.

Chamoli (960 m): Spiritual, scenic and absolutely splendid! Tucked into a bend of the River Alaknanda, Chamoli's hillsides are covered with forests of oak, birch, silver fir and pine brightened by incandescent Rhododendrons and wildflowers.

Exceptionally beautiful even in a region where nature's bounty is taken for granted, Chamoli is a great place to spend a few days in with comfortable hotels and rest houses, reasonably well stocked shops and decent dhabas and cafés. Chamoli was not always this travel-friendly. In the days of yore when folks said their final farewells before taking off for Badrinath, Chamoli was a wayside 'chatti' with little to offer but for a few ramshackle huts, a rough track and an insecure rope bridge. Luckily for the pilgrims, the British intervened, constructed a better bridge, rebuilt the road from Rishikesh, bulldozed the hillside flat and gave the chatti a fresh lease of life.

Antidote or Anecdote

Vishnu's faithful companion and vahana, the eagle Garuda, was left behind at Garuda Ganga while his lord and master went off to Badrinath. We presume that Garuda was not particularly dejected as he got by on a high protein diet of snakes, fav food of eagles.

The attention-grabbing angle on this tale is that post the Garuda sojourn, the pebbles at Garuda Ganga are supposed to have anti-snake and anti-scorpion properties. Not just do they keep out snakes and other venomous beasties but also work as a pretty effective antidote to snake/scorpion bites.

NB: We are definitely not recommending it as a remedy.

Joshimath (1890 m): Winter abode of Lord Badrinath, spiritual centre, adventure capital, army outpost, home of the National Institute of Mountaineering and tourist hub. How many caps can one place wear?

Joshimath was the first of the four maths established by the great Hindu philosopher saint and guru, Adi Shankaracharya, who attained enlightenment in these mountains. Befitting its status as a very holy city, Joshimath has its full complement of temples and shrines. Chief amongst them is the ancient Narsimha Temple built by King Lalitaditya of Kashmir in the 8th century. This temple is the seat of the Lord Badrinath in the winter months when the main shrine at Badri remains inaccessible.

Watch that Arm

Locals believe the arm of the idol of Vishnu Narsimha in the 1200-year-old temple at Joshimath is atrophying. When it finally breaks off, the mountains of Jai and Vijay at Vishnuprayag will collapse and block off the road to Badrinath.

NB: The shrine will reappear at Bhavishya Badri for the cosmic cycle of birth and death is eternal and endless.

Its religious importance aside, Joshimath is fast becoming an important tourist resort on account of its fantastic mountainscape, its great weather and the wealth of opportunities for adventure sport devotees. And like a self-respecting tourism centre, Joshimath has the requisite infrastructure to house, feed and entertain its guests.

Vishnuprayag (1372 m): The road from Joshimath winds its way towards Badrinath but first calls at Vishnuprayag, the first of the Panch Prayags. The turbulent Alaknanda descending at a fast pace, bursting with volume and vigour links up with its quieter sibling, the Dhauli Ganga at Vishnuprayag. Across the deep gorge where the Alaknanda and Dhauli Ganga celebrate their union with such high spirits, is a suspension bridge that certainly does not look safe enough to cross, but actually is.

Beyond lies the shrine of Badrinath enfolded by tiers and tiers of towering mountain ranges whose facades reflect the changing moods of the Sun God. To the east of Vishnuprayag looms the menacing grey and snowy white Nanda Devi (8106 m), beautiful, dangerous and absolutely irresistible.

Badrinath (3096 m): The road between Joshimath and Badrinath, only open between 06:00 hrs and 16:30 hrs, is so constricted by the mountains and the River Alaknanda, that it perforce follows

Blame it on Narada Muni

An unhealthy percentage of Hindu shrines are located in places so inaccessible that pilgrimages to them become do-or-die journeys. For the inapproachability of Badrinath, Hindus can thank Narada Muni, who chanced upon Vishnu enjoying the joys of domesticity. Being Narada, he could not leave well alone and chided the Lord for succumbing to worldly pleasures. Eschewing his wife Laxmi and all other comforts, Vishnu became an ascetic, took off for the most out-of-the-way place in the highest of mountains and lived off berries (badris). Poor Laxmi begged her Lord and Master to return to her, only to be told that he would if the valley of Badrinath remained a place for meditation and not worldly pleasures, and if he were worshipped in both 'yogic' and 'sringaric' forms.

So now, Vishnu and Laxmi are worshipped, not as husband and wife but as individual deities and the Rawal (head priest) of the Badrinath shrine has to be a Namboodri Brahmin from Kerala and celibate to boot. And all because of Narada!

a gate system which permits one single stream of vehicular traffic to ascend or descend at a time.

Badrinath's main shrine on the banks of the Alaknanda is attributed to Adi Shankaracharya and was built in the 9th century. The 15 m tall temple adheres to the proscribed rules of Hindu temple architecture and has three main sections – the sabha mandapam where devotees congregate, the darshana mandapam where rituals are performed and the garba griham or sanctum housing a black stone idol of Vishnu as Badrinath in a meditative pose. Close to the temple complex is a sacred tank of hot spring water for ablutions, a platform for performing rites, a rock with the impression of a serpent and a stone bearing the imprint of Vishnu's feet.

The season for the shrine is between April and November with the gates of the temple closing on Vijaya Dashmi, the 10th and final day of the Dussehra festival. Accommodation in tourist bungalows, dharamshalas and cottages operated and managed by the temple authorities is available at Badrinath. Non-vegetarian food and alcohol is taboo and even brandy for medicinal purpose is strictly no-can-do.

Return Leg

It's a one-way road to and from Badrinath. So either go back to Delhi via Joshimath, Devaprayag and Rishikesh or start walking towards the Valley of Flowers and the Sikh shrine of Hemkund Sahib.

ASIDES: SIDE BY SIDE

Alkapuri Glacier (6067 m, 15 km from Badrinath): Source of the mighty River Alaknanda and the abode of Kuber, god of wealth, celestial beings like Gandharvas and sundry yakshis and yakshganas.

Auli (2750 m, 8 km): The ski capital of India. Firmly packed snow, great slopes and good facilities for skiing or staying over.

Birahi (1100 m, 8 km from Chamoli): Another confluence! This time round, the Birahi Ganga meets the Alaknanda. But before it does that, the Birahi Ganga tumbles its way down from Gohna Tal, a beautiful water body that mirrors to perfection the snow-clad Nanda Ghunti Peak (6310 m).

Dewalgarh (19 km from Srinagar): Another temple in the mountains but one worth the detour.

Gohna Tal: Great Angling! Soil erosion and ravages of time may have reduced this vast lake's size but its beauty remains unsurpassed as do the Himalayan trout that live in its icy waters.

Gopeshwar (1515 m, 11 km from Chamoli): Chamoli district headquarters on the motorable road that connects Chamoli to Okhimath via Chopta. Picturesque surroundings and great climate and accommodation.

Helang (1524 m, 20 km from Pipalkoti): Turn left at Helang for the Panch Kedar shrine of Kapaleshwar in the beautiful Urgam Valley.

Hemkund Sahib (4329 m, 24 km from Govindghat): Sacred to both Sikhs and Hindus, the lake and temple complex at Hemkund has a gurudwara dedicated to Guru Gobind Singh and a temple to Laxmana, brother of Rama.

Kanatal (2575 m, 15 km from Chamba): A resort on the Chamba-Mussoorie Road, set in the midst of apple orchards and Himalayan views.

Khirsoo (300 m, 17 km from Srinagar): Perfect locale for quiet holidays in the midst of apple orchards, green fields, oak and deodar forests against a background of snow-capped Himalayan Ranges. Accommodation is available at GMVN Tourist Bungalow and Forest Rest House.

Mana (3 km from Badrinath): Home of the semi-nomadic Indo-Mongolian Mana tribe and last village 6.5 km short of India's border with Tibet.

Pipalkoti (1219 m, 10 km from Birahi): Hotels, dharamshalas, GMVN Tourist Bungalow and Forest Rest Houses provide ample accommodation in this large town on the way to Joshimath.

Satopanth Tal (4402 m, 25 km from Badrinath): Hinduism's Holy Trinity meditated at the three corners of this triangular glacial lake at the foot of Swargarohan Mt, a seven-stepped snow-clad mountain that is believed to be the staircase to heaven!

Tapovan (3798 m, 20 km from Joshimath): On the trekking trail to Bhavishya Badri, this glorious green valley, fertile and densely forested and beautified by mountain streams and hot springs, is the chosen destination of ascetics and recluses. Equally popular with regular folks looking for a quiet retreat.
Valley of Flowers (42 km from Badrinath): National Park along the course of the River Pushpawati where countless varieties and hues of wildflowers bloom between July and August.
Vasundhara Falls (5.5 km from Badrinath): The Alaknanda falls from a height of 122 m to create an exquisitely beautiful fairy tale waterfall.

TRAIL V: DELHI-MUNSIYARI

A roller coaster of a route to the beautiful Kumaoni hill resort of Munsiyari, a secretive, hush-hush kind of place hidden by tall mountains and dense forests from all but a few well-informed folks. And wouldn't they have loved to keep it that way. But luckily for the rest of us, television, travelogues, travel channels and tour operators brought Munsiyari into the limelight and now the road to Munsiyari is (almost but not quite) a well-trodden one!

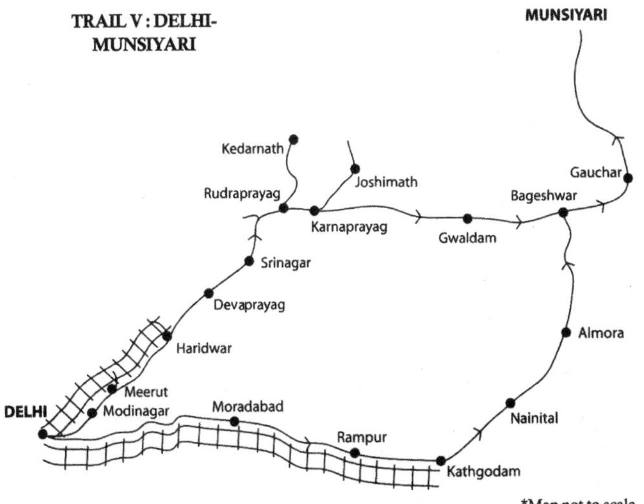

*Map not to scale

Travel this road to discover the Kumaon that lies hidden in mist shrouded valleys crammed with fruit orchards, terraced fields and stepped villages, and to meet its people – old men with furrowed faces, reticent young women and rosy cheeked, runny nosed brats.

The Routes

Delhi-Munsiyari via Haridwar and Bageshwar 665 km

Delhi→203 km→Haridwar→ 138 km→ Srinagar→ 66km→ Karnaprayag→70 km → Gwaldam → 46 km→Bageshwar→142 km→ Munsiyari

Delhi-Munsiyari via Kathgodam 567 km

Delhi→285 km→Kathgodam→ 90 km→Almora→64 km→ Rameshwar→73 km→Chaukori→ 75 km→Munsiyari

Trail Time: 17.5 hours of steady driving via Haridwar vis-a-vis 17 hours by way of Kathgodam. Add on time for lunch, tea and loo breaks, depending on the kind of family you are – if multiple halts are the norm, then plan on an overnight stop at Gwaldam or Almora. If you are the one-long-haul-and-then-let's-relax kind of folks, then you can do it in one go.

Follow the Road

Delhi-Haridwar: 203 km (4 hrs)
Haridwar-Srinagar: 138 km (3 hrs)
Srinagar-Karnaprayag: 66 km (2 hrs)
Karnaprayag-Gwaldam: 70 km (2 hrs)
Gwaldam-Bageshwar: 46 km (1.5 hrs)
Bageshwar-Munsiyari: 142 km (5-6 hrs)
Delhi-Kathgodam: 285 km (6 hrs)
Kathgodam-Almora: 90 km (3 hrs)
Almora-Rameshwar: 64 km (2 hrs)
Rameshwar-Chaukori: 73 km (3 hrs)
Chaukori-Munsiyari: 75 km (3 hrs)

Escape Plan

A drive at night in the Indian hills is never a good idea, so skip the sleep, get up with the larks and out of Delhi city while the going is good. Both routes take a fair bit of time and involve a goodly length of mountain roads, so an early morning getaway is highly recommended.

Other Ways to Do It

Take a flight to Jolly Grant Airport, Dehradun or settle for a train ride to Kathgodam or Haridwar and then cab, car or bus the rest of the distance by way of the high road to Munsiyari via Almora or Bageshwar.

Stopovers

Kathgodam: A grimy, dirt encrusted, dusty little town with little going for it except that it is the railhead for Kumaon. And even the poky, soporific Railway Station wears a 'my days are over' air. Still, trains do come from and go back to Delhi, Lucknow, Kolkata and Agra (why Agra?) though rarely on schedule, and when they do, the Station Master stirs himself to re-assert his authority over the few coolies, the sorry potted plant, the odd linesmen, the solitary sweeper and the long-suffering passengers squatting on his platform. Just outside, lying in wait for the new arrivals are the touts for the taxi, bus, hotel and dhaba operators annoyingly loud in their eagerness to drum up business and grab the unsuspecting traveller.

Nainital (1938 m): India's Lake District. Long, long ago there were over sixty lakes nestling in grassy hollows surrounded by tall pines and stately oaks and enfolded by even taller mountains. Sadly very few survived the pressures of time but the ones that have are absolute gems. Best known of them all is the emerald green Naini Lake, an iridescent gemstone whose beauty is enhanced by its setting. Naini Lake is the fulcrum around which Nainital revolves. Named after the temple dedicated to Naina Devi (Goddess Parvati) whose eye is believed to have fallen here, Nainital has long been a convenient and cool place to spend the summer months. It still remains an absolutely delightful place despite the crowds of tourists that choke the Mall, clog the streets and hog up its hotels.

The other lakes in close proximity to Nainital include Bhim Tal (22 km), the biggie of them all; the nine-cornered Naukuchiya Tal (4 km from Bhim Tal); the anglers' paradise at Khurpatal (12 km) and the seven little lakes at Sat Tal (23 km). Easily accessible by road, the lakes support small settlements, which cater to the influx of tourists. Cottages on sprawling estates, lakeside resorts, tourist bungalows and small hotels provide a variety of accommodation and in common with most places in India, plenty of small cafés and dhabas to eat in.

Almora (1646 m): Not far from crowded Nainital is its quieter and more serene cousin, Almora. Perched on a five km long saddle shaped ridge between the Rivers Kosi and Suyal, Almora was a celebrated centre for Kumaoni culture and crafts. Blessed with a scenic locale and excellent climate, Almora flourished as the capital of Chand Rajas of Kumaon. It enjoyed a revival when the British realized its merit as an R & R destination. So up they came, built sanatoriums and hospitals, convinced Almora's cool climes and clean air would cure them of the tropical ailments endemic to the subcontinent. Not that all of them recovered, judging by the numbers that are buried in the cemetery at Almora. Still, Almora remains the hotspot for a cool interlude.

Srinagar (1646 m): Ambitious, hopeful and desirous of being the

Bal Mithai – the Kumaonese Truffle

Take a kilo of condensed milk (khoya), cook it over a slow flame till it becomes a glorious brown and looks more chocolate than milk. Add 400 gms of sugar; stir some more so the sugar dissolves into the khoya. Pour into a well greased tray – cut into squares when set. Now comes the best part – toss each square in a bowl of silver balls till well coated – all silver and no fudge.

Voila! We present Bal Mithai, Kumaon's answer to chocolate truffles!

PS: An even easier way to get a plateful of Bal Mithai is to simply walk into any sweet shop – this particular sweetmeat is readily available across the length and breadth of Kumaon.

capital of Uttaranchal, Srinagar is holding its breath waiting for boom time. Meanwhile, it grows unfettered into a sprawling mess of a city with every little flat patch of land abloom with construction sites.

Karnaprayag (832 m): The confluence of the Alaknanda and the Pindar takes place at Karnaprayag, one of the five holy prayags or confluences where the different streams of the Ganga unite into one powerful river before entering the plains. The best accommodation in Karnaprayag is available at the GMVN Tourist Complex Rishilok.

Legend & Lore

Eons ago when the Himalayas were the realm of the sadhus and sages, Karan, the son of Kunti (also mother of the Pandavas from the epic Mahabharata) came to the place that now bears his name, Karnaprayag, to pray and meditate and thereby invoke the blessings of his celestial father Surya. Pleased with Karan's integrity, generosity and valour, Surya granted him the boon of an impregnable shield that guaranteed his invincibility. Unfortunately for Karan, his mother asked him to give his shield to his younger half-brother Arjuna and generous to the end, Karan did so only to be vanquished and slain in battle by the very same brother.

Gwaldam (1829 m): Straddling the Garhwal and Kumaon districts of Uttaranchal, Gwaldam marries the scenic splendours of one with the serenity of the other. Just a little distance off the main road, Gwaldam is a pastoral idyll of whispering pine forests, tinkling rivulets, apple orchards and meadows filled with wild gladioli, briar roses and daisies.

Gwaldam offers what are, without

exception, the best views of Nanda Devi and Trishul and of the panorama of the Greater Himalayan Range. KMVN Tourist Bungalow, Forest and PWD Rest Houses provide ample accommodation for the few who venture this way.

The Lake of Skeletons

Hundreds of skeletal remains of men and animals were found at the beautiful alpine lake at Roopkund (4500 m), 60 km ahead of Gwaldam. One version has it that this is what happened to the army of the legendary Dogra General Zorawar Singh who disappeared in 1841 whilst on a military campaign to conquer Tibet.

Bageshwar (975 m): The Rivers Saryu and Gomti converge in this town that has an impressive historical and religious lineage dating back to Puranic era. Associated with Lord Shiva who roamed this area as a lion, (Bagh=Lion + Ishwar= God adds up to Bageshwar) Bageshwar has an ancient Shiva Temple and celebrates its association with the god during the annual Uttaraini Fair (January) and at Shivaratri (Feb/March).

For the trail, it's another place to tank up on food and fuel but for the adventurous, Bageshwar is the launch pad for treks to the glaciers at Sunderdunga, Pindari and Kafni. KMVN Tourist Bungalow, Forest and PWD Rest Houses provide reasonably priced accommodation, the other option being the small hotels in Bageshwar.

Munsiyari (2290 m): If the essence of Kumaon Himalayas could be contained in one place, then in Munsiyari it is. Roseate dawns and crimson sunsets sprinkle colour upon the snowy white summits of the Greater Himalayas, dark green pine and deodar forests are illuminated from within by pink, white and red flowering rhododendrons and silver streams the Gori Ganga as it cascades and spills its way downhill creating rapids and pools that even-handedly delight river rafters and anglers. Further ahead lie the Milam, Namik and Ralam glaciers. Solitude, serenity and tranquility are the USP of this tiny little town tucked away at the foot of the Panchchhuli Range (6437 m). Swiss cottages (tents) at the Wayfarer Resort are the other accommodation available apart from the KMVN and Forest Rest Houses.

Back Home

What goes up certainly comes down, as does the road to Munsiyari. And that is certainly the easiest way to get back to where it all began. But for those who prefer variations on the same theme, we recommend that if you have followed one route up, take the other one down. That way, you get to see a little more of scenic wonderland that is Uttaranchal.

Salt Route to Tibet

The pucca road ends at Munsiyari and beyond it lies the rough track that marks one of the major trading routes into Tibet. The semi-nomadic Shauka/Bhutiya tribesmen of Indo-Tibetan origin took yak trains laden with grain and factory goods, which they traded for salt, borax, and turquoise that were then sold across the length and breadth of the Indian Himalayas. The Indo-China war of 1962 put paid to this happy state of affairs when the border areas were declared off limits and the mountain passes between India and Tibet closed off.

ASIDES: SIDE BY SIDE

Baijnath (1125 m, 61 km from Almora): Capital of the Katyuri dynasty, remnants of its former grandeur can be seen in the temple complex on the banks of the River Gomti.

Binsar (2310 m, 30 km from Almora): Relatively unknown but still has a large resort complex to provide creature comforts. Surrounded by thick forests of oak and rhododendron, Binsar sits on a ridge with spectacular views of the Almora Valley on one side and the steep Himalayan Ranges on the other.

Bhim Tal (1371 m, 22 km from Nainital): Great for a day trip or an overnight halt at this beautiful mountain lake with an island that boasts a café.

Chaukori (2010 m, 93 km from Almora): Nature rules. Tea gardens, woods, streams and sparkling snow-clad mountains in Chaukori in the heart of Kumaon with panoramic views of the Himalayas. KMVN Tourist Bungalow and Lodge provide the accommodation.

Jageshwar (1900 m, 36 km from Almora): 124 temples, innumerable finely crafted statues, two rivers and one of twelve Jyotirlingas make this one of the holiest places in Kumaon.

Kausani (1890 m, 44 km from Almora): Watch the sun appear over the Himalayan peaks in this pretty resort also known as the Switzerland of Kumaon.

Kilbury (2528 m, 12 km from Nainital): Great for weekends, camping and bird-watching with beautiful views of Terai and Bhabar below.

Malla Ramgarh (35 km from Nainital): The fruit basket of Kumaon, this lovely valley lives in the shadow of the magnificent Nanda Devi and Trishul peaks. Pretty cottages and well-equipped campsite make this a great place to restore those jaded spirits.

Mukteshwar (2300 m, 45 km from Nainital): A small hill station in the middle of dense forests is home to the Indian Veterinary Institute. It offers restorative walks, solitude, flora and fauna and views of the Himalayas right up to the Adi Nampa Peak in Nepal.

Mundoli (1750 m, 24 km from Gwaldam): On the trekking trail to the alpine meadows of Ali Bugyal (3275 m) and Bedni Bugyal (3554 m).

Naukuchiya Tal (1218 m, 4 km from Bhim Tal): Isolated from the rest of the world by dense forests, this nine-cornered lake is fast becoming a very popular resort. Perfect for angling, walks and general R & R.

Patal Bhubhaneshwar (110 km from Almora): Underground tunnel leads to the cave temple of Patal Bhubhaneshwar dedicated to 33 crore deities. The temple has magnificent carvings of the Hindu pantheon as well as of flora and fauna of the region.

Ranikhet (1830 m, 63 km from Nainital): Beautifully simple or simply beautiful! Meadows, cedar and pine forests and fab views of the snow covered Himalayas. This old British garrison town retains its personality and character – church, golf course and old soldiers et al. Pleasant accommodation and good food assist to make it a perfect holiday.

Roopkund (4478 m, 60 km from Gwaldam): High-altitude lake in the midst of the snow-covered Himalayas with picture-perfect views of Nandaghunti (6309 m), Nanda Devi (7817 m), Trishul (7120 m) and Chaukhamba (7838 m).

TRAIL VI: DELHI-DHARCHULA

Nandadevi, Nandakot, Nandakhat, Trishul, Panchchhuli, Hardeol, Rajrambha, Bambadhura and Basuli Danda – these snow-crested invincible mountain peaks, the ultra superior members of the Greater Himalayas, stand like a protective phalanx guarding the treasures that lie in valleys below. Once out of bounds because of its proximity to India's borders with China and Tibet, this part of Kumaon is quickly becoming a favourite destination with the traveller looking for more from a holiday than what the average hill station churns out by default.

Dharchula, Pithoragarh and Champawat steal the hearts of those ready to brave some jolting and jostling along a not-so-great road, ordinary rooms and everyday kind of cuisine for a terrain where glaciers dissolve into torrential rivers, snow-covered mountains wear the colours of the sun, bare hillsides bloom with rhododendrons and lush valleys riot with flowers and fruits come summer.

TRAIL VI : DELHI-DHARCHULA

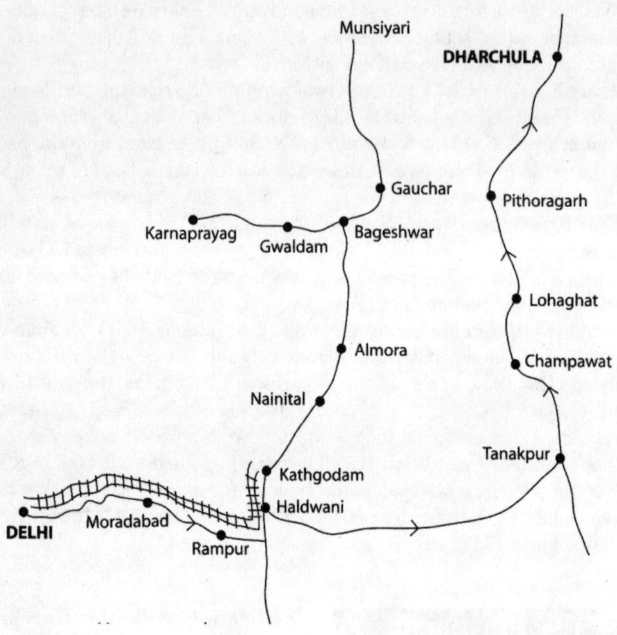

*Map not to scale

The Route: 630 km

Delhi→280 km→Haldwani→ 109 km→Tanakpur→75 km→ Champawat→80 km→Pithoragarh →87 km→Dharchula

Trail Time: 20 hrs of driving, the last 180 km on a mountain road that leaves much to be desired. So plan an overnight halt or short stay at Champawat, Lohaghat or Abbot Mount before conquering the trail's

Follow the Road

Delhi-Haldwani: 280 km (6-7 hrs) (via Moradabad and Rampur)
Haldwani-Tanakpur: 109 km (4 hrs)
Tanakpur-Champawat: 75 km (2 hrs)
Champawat-Pithoragarh: 80 km (3 hrs)
Pithoragarh-Dharchula: 87 km (4-5 hrs)

summit at Dharchula. The accommodation available in this part of Kumaon is very basic – no frills and no fancy fittings but at prices that are hard to beat.

Stopovers

Follow Trail VII till Haldwani but dump it when it turns for Kathgodam. Trail VI will beat its own path to Tanakpur via Chorgalya, the first stop on its way to the beautiful Saur Valley.

Get Moving

There are always more ways of reaching a destination than one. So if driving in the mountains is not your idea of a holiday, it's fine because there are others who will happily do it for you. Rent a car or MUV in Delhi, pack in the troops, show the driver the green light and sit back to savour the drive in style. Alternately, take a train to Kathgodam or Tanakpur, the nearest railhead for Pithoragarh. Trains connect Tanakpur to Lucknow and Delhi, Kolkata and Lucknow to Kathgodam. Cabs and KMMOU buses are available outside the railway stations. Just haggle your way to the right price and you are on your way up!

Tanakpur: An obscure little border town on the banks of the River Sarda, which begins life in a glacier near the sacred Lake Mansarovar at the foot of the holy Mt Kailash in Tibet. The Sarda is a river that goes by many names – Kali when it enters Indian space, Sarda in the lower reaches of Kumaon and Ghaghra in Bihar, just before it flows into the Ganga and is thereafter known as Ganga. Tanakpur was established by the British way back in 1880 – why they chose to do so remains a matter of speculation for the town has nothing going for it.

Still Tanakpur is as good a place as any to begin the ascent into the Himalayan heights and having been through it, one values the sparkling clean air and splendid scenery even more.

Champawat (1615 m): Lord Vishnu chose this little mofussil town to make his appearance on earth in his Kurma (tortoise) avatar. It's true except that when Vishnu came, there was no seedy little town cluttered with homes and buildings, the bare hills were covered with dense green forests and governance was a thing left to kings and courtiers, not democratically elected men with abysmal taste in architecture and furnishing! Check out the Tourist Bungalow if you still won't believe us! Rooms at KMVN Tourist Bungalow need to be booked well in advance as the demand exceed the supply.

Actually, till democracy and modernization began to extract their pounds of flesh from Champawat, it was full of dark forests wherein roamed tigers whose idea of a gourmet meal was to masticate on a man or two. That is, till Jim Corbett decided to write 'The Man Eater of Champawat' and hunted them all down!

During its heyday as the capital of the Chand dynasty, Champawat was transformed into a royal city adorned with exquisitely carved wood and stone temples dedicated to the region's ruling deity, Shiva, and his consort, Parvati. The Nagnath Temple where Shiva is enshrined as Lord of Serpents and the 1000-year-old Baleshwar Temple complex are prime examples of the skill and effort that went into the ornate and elaborately carved panels and figures used to decorate the temples.

Lohaghat (1750 m): In common with most parts of Kumaon, Lohaghat too has a history richly steeped in colourful incidents from Hindu religion and mythology. As per the Krishna Leela, Krishna vanquished the thousand-armed demon Banasura in Lohaghat – adding substance to this myth is the ruined fortress where Banasura is believed to have confined Krishna's grandson Aniruddha.

Bear in mind that looks are deceptive and remember to never judge a book by its cover and you will believe us when we tell you that Lohaghat was a thriving centre for trade and commerce in the not-so-distant past till Indo-Chinese relations plummeted into a black hole and took with them Lohaghat's prosperity. Today, the folks of Lohaghat earn whatever money they can from the iron implements they craft so well. Alternately, they make money off the tourists who pass by their town – they feed them and house them and even guide them.

Pithoragarh (1815 m): It's only when the road nears Pithoragarh that the trail begins to justify its existence. Living under the watchful gaze of Nanda Devi, Trishul, Nandakhat, Rajrambha, Panchchhuli and other Himalayan peaks, Pithoragarh is often compared to Kashmir and why not? Forests of pine, rhododendron, oak, cedar and cypress thin out into alpine meadows (bugyals) that in

Do Unto Others, as You Would Have Them Do Unto You

The hapless victim of a conspiracy hatched by his stepmother, Goril, a young Katyuri prince was locked into an iron cage and flung into the river. Idolized by his subjects for his integrity, sense of justice and righteousness, the young prince was immortalized as Gwal Devta and enshrined in a temple built in his honour. Thousands of pilgrims throng his temple at Golchaurh in Champawat hoping to receive their dues from the God of Justice. As in life, so too in death and deification, the prince dispenses justice and thus lives up to his name and fame!

summer are spangled with wildflowers. In its higher altitude areas are the glaciers of Milam, Namik, Ralam, Meola and Balati while lower down frolic the Rivers Kuti, Dhauli Ganga, Gori Ganga, Ram Ganga, Saryu and Kali creating perfect conditions for a host of water sports.

That was the district of Pithoragarh, now for the town, which is of more immediate importance. Tucked into a narrow alley of a valley barely 5 km by 2 km, Pithoragarh town grew from a fortified stronghold of the Chand Rajas into an important outpost on the trade routes to Nepal, China and Tibet. The Chinese aggression in 1962 put paid to trade and now Pithoragarh does duty as a garrison town keeping a wary eye on the Chinese troops across the border. Trade routes aside, for devout Hindus, Pithoragarh was the last big settlement on the extremely sacrosanct (and strenuous) pilgrimage to Kailash-Mansarovar in Tibet.

Pithoragarh has a goodly number of hotels, tourist bungalows and rest houses that cater to an increasing number of tourists and adventure enthusiasts who flock here. Apart from climbing, trekking and angling, Pithoragarh abounds in locales perfect for river rafting, canoeing, kayaking, hang-gliding and skiing and is just about beginning to realize its potential with the help of Uttaranchal Ministry of Tourism and the Kumaon Mandal Vikas Nigam.

Dharchula (6151 m): Stark brown slopes bereft of vegetation, piles of rubble along the road and the rock-strewn riverbed of the River Kali serve as silent but effective reminders that this is a landslide-prone area in the seismically volatile Himalayas. Barely 60 km away is the village of Malpa, the scene of the horrific landslide of August 1998 that claimed the lives of 60 pilgrims undertaking the hazardous Kailash-Mansarovar Yatra. Like Pithoragarh, Dharchula has long been a routine stop on the traditional trekking route to Kailash-Mansarovar as well as on the trade routes to Tibet and Nepal. Nepal lies on the other side of the River Kali, whose fast flowing, icy waters form a natural and very effective barrier between the two countries. Accommodation is available in Dharchula at KMVN Tourist Hut, NPHC, PWD Rest House and small privately-owned lodges – though they all lose out to the hospitality offered by the troops stationed at Dharchula.

Homeward Bound

Choose from two options – the first one takes the way down past Pithoragarh, Champawat and Tanakpur to Haldwani, Ramnagar, Moradabad and finally Delhi. Or try the one that travels from Pithoragarh to Almora (118 km via Rameshwar, Dhyari, Danya, Suakhan and Bare Chhina) and meets up the original trail at Haldwani after travelling via Nainital and Kathgodam.

Shiva's Tandav or Man's Folly?

In a different era, the earth trembled and shook when an enraged Shiva performed the Tandav Nritya, the Cosmic Dance of Destruction, and men and gods cringed, helpless in the face of such earth-shattering fury. As they still do when the earth moves, hills crumple, rocks tumble and walls of mud and water wash away everything in their path.

In our times, rampant felling of trees all along the Himalayas has caused severe soil erosion, so much so that when it rains, landslides become routine, mountainsides are washed away in torrents of mud that clog rivers, forcing them to alter their course. The greed to grow cash crops like rice in place of traditional soil-binding crops like millet on terraced fields shorn of any grass or tree cover further weakens the porous slopes. Fuelling this Himalayan tragedy is the unhindered construction of dams, roads and buildings with little care of their impact on this seismically unstable region. So, when you travel in Uttaranchal, spare a thought for this ecologically volatile land that is as fragile as it is beautiful.

ASIDES: SIDE BY SIDE

Abbot Mount (15 km from Lohaghat): The most exclusive and idyllic hill resort in Kumaon, standing in the middle of oak and deodar, was first settled by a British gentleman way back in 1914. KMVN is working on making Abbot Mount a tourist centre for adventure sports. The best accommodation available is in the British Raj-vintage bungalows, most of them now privately-owned. So pull out the stops and contact old pals of old pals who have a place here!

Ascot Sanctuary (42 km from Dharchula): Glacial amphitheatres, ridges, spurs, valleys and riverbeds make up the 284 sq km sanctuary whose primary aim is to protect and conserve the elusive and endangered musk deer. Forest and PWD Rest House at Ascot provide the sole accommodation.

Chipla Kedar (4626 m, 53 km from Dharchula): Trekkers' delight and a visual treat for all others with absolutely exquisite views of the Himalayas.

Devidhura (2500 m, 58 km from Tanakpur): An annual fair is held on Rakshabandhan (August) at the temple dedicated to Goddess Barahi Devi.

Didihat (1850 m, 54 km from Pithoragarh): Stop here for the very best views of the Himalayan Panorama.

Gangolighat (77 km from Pithoragarh): Shiva and Kali Temple town is the venue of annual fairs during the Navratras (March/April and October). Further ahead lies the unusual underground temple of Patal Bhubhaneshwar dedicated to 33 crore deities!

Jaul Jibi (29 km from Dharchula): Indo-Nepal border town on the confluence of Rivers Gori and Kali – stop only if you want to buy some Made in China stuff. Take off point for trekking trails along River Gori Ganga towards Milam Glacier (3423 m) and to Lipu La (5344 m) along the River Kali.

Mayawati (1940 m, 22 km from Champawat): The 104-year-old headquarters of the Adwaita Ashram promises solitude and serenity at Mayawati, a name given by Swami Vivekanand in 1901. For accommodation (3 nights only), write to President, Adwaita Ashram, Mayawati, PO Lohaghat, Pithoragarh – 262524.

Narayan Swami Ashram (23 km from Dharchula): The ashram on the banks of the River Kali provides the perfect ambience for meditation and spiritual edification.

Purnagiri (20 km from Tanakpur): Built by the Raja of Kumaon in the 15th century, the temple atop the Purnagiri Hill commemorates the spot where the Goddess Parvati's navel fell. The last steep and rough stretch of 8 km through dense forests is done on foot. Dharamshalas and KMVN lodge provide basic accommodation during the yatra (March-April and October).

Shyamtal (6 km from Sukhidhung): The ashram of Swami Birajnanda stands on a 300-acre estate packed with pine, deodar, teak, cherry, magnolia and eucalyptus trees. It gets its name from the three beautiful little lakes near the ashram. The ashram has a guesthouse but no frills and no electricity either. For bookings, write to President, Vivekananda Ashram, PO Sukhidhung, Pithoragarh-262523.

TRAIL VII: DELHI-ALMORA VIA NAINITAL & RANIKHET

Sweeping their way up from the fertile plains of Terai and Bhabar into the skyline are the Greater Himalayas, the awesome mountain range that forms a natural barrier between India and Central Asia. The Greater Himalayas bequeath to Kumaon an unsurpassed bounty of natural beauty that encompasses mountains over 6000 m, swift-flowing rivers that cascade their way downhill, jewel-like lakes crowded with silver fish, dense forests of sweet-scented pines, verdant valleys lush with ripening crops and weather that

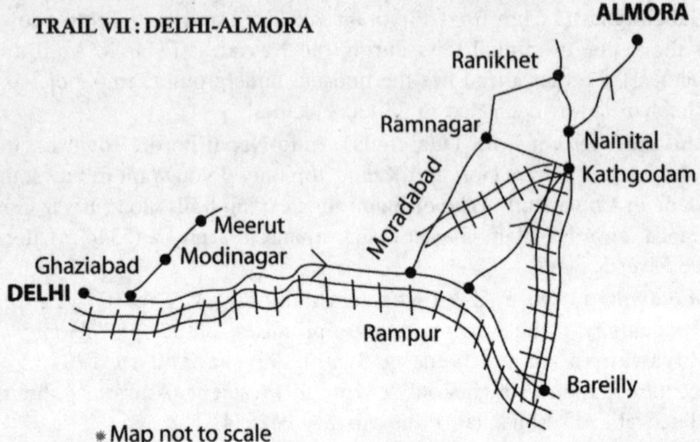

is to die for, especially when the mercury is rising in the plains.

So divinely beautiful and blessed is Kumaon that the locals decided to keep it to themselves and who can blame them? Way back in the early years of the 19th century, British explorers looking to develop and document this wonderful region were habitually sent off on wild goose chases by the clever Kumaoni. And like any other secret, the tales of Kumaon grew in the telling till the British aptitude to 'go anywhere, do anything' finally found Kumaon a place on the map. Our trail takes travellers into the best-developed hinterland of Kumaon, to its most popular hill resorts of Nainital, Ranikhet and Almora.

The Route: 426 km

Delhi→285 km→Kathgodam→35 km → Nainital → 59 km→ Ranikhet→ 47 km→Almora

Follow the Road

Delhi-Kathgodam: 285 km (6-7 hrs)
Kathgodam-Nainital: 35 km (1 hr)
Nainital-Ranikhet: 59 km (2 hr)
Ranikhet-Almora: 47 km (1.5 hrs)

Trail Time: 10-11 hours of steady driving at a comfortable speed of 50 kmph is all you need to accomplish to arrive at trail's end at Almora. This point-to-point time schedule is worked out without giving due consideration to the imponderables – traffic glitches, breakdowns, inordinately long or frequent stops.

Stopovers

On its way to Kathgodam, National Highway 24 passes through the archetypal Uttar Pradesh towns of Ghaziabad, Roorkee, Moradabad,

Get Started

Wake up bright and early to beat Delhi's appalling traffic before it can get to you. Or if you are an impenitent late riser, then settle for the overnight train ride from Delhi to Kathgodam. The train arrives at a not too unreasonable hour of the morning, at which stage, you can climb out and negotiate your way to the right price with the local cab operator and take off for Almora. Alternately, catch the bus up to Nainital, Ranikhet or Almora. A number of day/overnight deluxe and ordinary buses ply between Delhi and Kathgodam, Nainital, Almora or Ranikhet.

Hapur, Gajraula and Rampur, where the air is thick with a heady cocktail of warm molasses mixed with the outpouring of industrial effluents. This is UP's sugarcane belt, prosperous, regressive and notorious in equal measure. The first is highly visible in the arrogant mien of the men folk, in their kitschy houses and in the sugarcane laden tractor-trolleys that refuse to give way. Less tangible but very much there is the chauvinism, casteism and parochialism. Finally the notoriety –criminals rule the road and don't pull their shots once the sun sets, so much so that no underwriter would risk his money on the foolish one who chooses to do this stretch of the highway after dark. So make sure this section of the trail is done in the company of other vehicular traffic, if not in broad daylight.

The quickest get away is by bypassing them altogether. While there is no escaping the miasma of small town Uttar Pradesh, two new bypasses at Hapur and Moradabad at least spare travellers the pits and potholes of these two towns. The first break for a meal or refreshments can be at the Mid Way Café after Gajraula, another of UP's sugar towns with nothing sweet about it, or at any one of the numerous dhabas flanking the highway. Gauge the popularity of a dhaba by the number of charpoys positioned outside it. If a truckie likes a dhaba, he will not just eat at it but also grab some much needed shut eye, so stake out the one with the maximum number of stringed cots in its front yard.

The trail says goodbye to NH 24 at Rampur, the erstwhile kingdom of the Nawabs of Rampur celebrated for its culture, cuisine and bloodhounds. Those with the time and the inclination can and should stop by at Rampur's Raza Library with its outstanding collection of 12,000 rare manuscripts and Mughal miniature paintings.

The well-maintained highway becomes a has-been as the road, now reduced to a state highway, dashes off towards Rudrapur, and thereafter begins its approach towards Haldwani, Kathgodam and Nainital, Queen of the Kumaon.

Nainital (1938 m): The road winds

forward flanked by the tops of pine and deodar trees rising from the floor of the valley below where strawberry fields and mulberry trees produce the bounty sold in pretty little cane baskets all the way up to Nainital.

Nainital is a splendid hill station sprawling around its centrepiece, the absolutely exquisite Naini Lake, that never fails to elicit gasps of delight, despite the attrition that threatens its size and beauty. As its main thoroughfare, the Mall Road curves up from Tallital, the point of entry into Nainital with its crowded bus stand and cab ranks towards Mallital, the commercial heart of the resort, and before you unfolds the glorious sight of red, blue, green and white striped sails of yachts skimming over the dazzling blue waters of Naini Lake.

The lake lies in the protective embrace of the seven mountains that sweep up from the very edge of the water creating an amphitheatre that has been grossly overused by developers looking to extract megabucks from every square yard of available space. Nowadays, the charming hill station of yore has become yet another victim of progress and is crowded, congested and highly commercialized but nevertheless manages to hold its own. All the action in Nainital happens around Mallital and the flat open area abutting the lake called what else but the Flats! The opposite shore of the lake is more exclusive with the Governor's mansion, deluxe hotels, residential schools and summer homes of the rich and not all that famous.

Like any self-respecting hill station, Nainital too provides its visitors a host of choices and opportunities. A plethora of lovely lakes, seven peaks, innumerable picnic sites, a self-important Yacht Club and plenty of shops and restaurants to wine, dine, shop, climb, sail, swim or fish.

Two Annas of Land

Mr Barron, the British entrepreneur responsible for 'discovering' Nainital in 1829, was one smart operator. Having heard about this jewel of a lake hidden in the Kumaon hills, he hired a guide and went looking for it. The guide, in common with other locals, was reluctant to lead outsiders to the place believed to be the abode of gods and so pretended not to know his way to the lake. At which point, the wily Englishman asked him to carry a load of rocks till they found the lake, as he intended to build a house there and had been told there were no stones around the lake. The rocks nearly broke the guide's back, as well as his spirit and the poor fella led Mr Barron straight to the Naini Lake. Mr Barron built himself a fine house on the shores of the lake, on land he leased for the princely sum of two annas! Real estate prices in Nainital have skyrocketed since, but Mr Barron's house still stands proud on its two annas worth of land.

Ranikhet (1830 m): 400 straight kilometres of snow-capped Himalayan Mountains welcome visitors to Ranikhet – the perfect place to escape when the commercialization of Nainital feels too crass! Development gave Ranikhet the go by, perhaps because its residents preferred it to do so or maybe because the Indian Army annexed a large chunk of Ranikhet for the Kumaon Regimental Centre! Whatever be the cause, visitors to Ranikhet unanimously applaud the decision to preserve the old-world ambience and the almost tangible aura of peace and tranquility. A holiday in Ranikhet is about long walks, priceless moments of solitude, quality family time and maybe a game of golf.

But wait. It's not as if time has passed Ranikhet by leaving it stuck in a time warp. The main market, the Sadar Bazaar, spread along the busy thoroughfare is a mind-numbing and ear-splitting cacophony of sound during the day when buses and cars charge through, blaring horns and blasting film music to announce their existence or their imminent arrival/departure. The only way to escape the din is to stay well away on the other quieter side of town

Here, the Mall Road wends its way to the prettier Ranikhet, the one with a close resemblance to the green glades that delighted Rani Padmini so much that they came to be known as the Queen's Field (Rani + Khet). This Ranikhet has old colonial buildings, an elegant stone church, curlicued narrow lanes winding their way up to pretty cottages sitting in flower-filled gardens, thick stands of deodar, oak and pine resonant with bird songs and air so clean and crisp that it invigorates and refreshes the spirit and the soul; small wonder, then, that a queen fell in love with this place and claimed it for her own.

Almora (1650 m): Remember reading those books on the Wild West where the 'sun rode low in the saddle of the hills'? Almora is actually situated on one such saddle lying between the Rivers Kosi and Suyal, extending over five kilometres along the Kashyap Hills. Almora preserves the rich cultural heritage of Kumaon that was at its zenith during the rule of the Chand dynasty (15th-18th century) before it first slipped into the hands of the Gurkhas and then the British.

Almora is truly the custodian of the best of Kumaonese culture, cuisine and crafts – streets paved with locally quarried stones run between traditional slate roofed houses embellished with ornate woodwork, and temples, forts, palaces and government buildings represent an era long gone but a culture very much alive.

Extremely hospitable, Almora offers visitors a good range of accommodation to choose from – Circuit house, PWD and Forest Rest Houses to KMVN Tourist Bungalow

Of Stamp Papers and Brass Bells

An 8 km long walk or horse cart ride through a forest smelling like good quality deodorant gets to the Chitai Temple whose walls are plastered with stamp papers with wishes on them. It is also crammed with bells donated by those whose wishes were fulfilled by Golju, a local god who certainly does a remarkably efficient job of wish fulfilment going by the hundreds and thousands of bells hanging in the temple premises.

as well as a goodly number of hotels. See Hotels in Almora for their names and numbers.

Return Leg

The easiest part of the trip – simply roll downhill the way you came up! Following the trail in reverse is the most convenient way to get back home but those with time to spare can think about returning home via the Corbett National Park. It takes 4 or 5 hrs to do the 96 km between Ranikhet and Ramnagar on a fairly good road that runs along the edge of the park and has a number of gates that allow entry into the Tiger Reserve. Hotels, lodges, log huts and guesthouses are available at Ramnagar and Dhikala. The Forest Department has 24 Rest Houses in the reserve, which can be booked through the Field Director's Office, Ramnagar.

ASIDES: SIDE BY SIDE

Binsar (2310 m, 30 km from Almora): Once the capital of the Chand Rajas, Binsar is now considered the capital of off-the-beaten-path holiday destinations.

Binsar Sanctuary: Temperate to sub-arctic climate. The 50 sq km of land in the Gananath Forest Reserve is home to high-altitude flora and fauna –oak, rhododendron, blue pine, spruce and birch, leopard, civet cats, serow, gharial, musk deer, Himalayan brown bear and Himalayan pheasants. The Binsar Valley Resort offers facilities for mountain biking, jeep safaris, camping and of course a roof over the guest's bed.

Chaubatia (9 km from Ranikhet): A charming little hamlet set in the midst of apple, apricot and peach orchards that are a visual treat in springtime. The KRC Museum here is worth a visit, especially if you are an old warhorse. 4 km ahead is Bhalu Dam, Ranikhet's water source and a good place for picnics.

Dwarahat (1540 m, 38 km from Ranikhet): 55 ancient temples (11-16th century) commemorate the site of the former capital of Kumaon's Katyuri dynasty. 10 km ahead is the Doonagiri Temple atop a hillock where the legendary life-saving Sanjivini herb of Ramayana, Hanuman and Laxmana fame is found.

Jalana (35 km from Almora): Another picturesque little township in the fruit-producing Katyur Valley with panoramic views of the mountains above and the vale below.

Katarmal (17 km from Almora): Come here to see the 800-year-old temple dedicated to Surya, the Sun God.

Kausani (1890 m, 44 km from Almora): So beautiful and tranquil that even Mahatma Gandhi succumbed to its charms.

The Lakes: Sat Tal, Bhim Tal, Naukuchiya Tal & Khurpa Tal – picture-perfect settings, comfortable accommodation, angling, boating and sightseeing, all within a 25 km radius from Nainital.

Manila (85 km from Ranikhet): Its name means enchantment. The Katyuri Kings certainly loved it for they built the family deity Manila Devi's temple here.

Mukteshwar (2290 m, 45 km from Nainital): An old hoary legend about a demon and Shiva, a hundred-year-old Shiva Temple, a modern resort complex and fabulous views of the peaks of Trishul, Nanda Devi, Neelkantha, Nandaghunti and the five Panchchhuli.

Shitlakhet (35 km from Ranikhet): A scenic spot with commanding views of the Himalayas, this is also the birthplace of Pt Gobind Ballabh Pant. Accommodation is available in modest hotels, KMVN Tourist Bungalow and Government Rest Houses. The surrounding forest abounds in medicinal plants and herbs, and hopefully some wild life too.

For other places in the vicinity of Nainital, Almora and Ranikhet, check out Asides listed in Trail V.

TRAIL VIII: DELHI-DHANAULTI VIA MUSSOORIE

This has to be a most redundant trail for it follows a path so well trodden that it qualifies as seriously trampled, flattened and beaten underfoot. Except for first timers, few are the folks who want to follow it anymore even though the mountains around Mussoorie hide myriad gems of destinations. Two such jewels being the little hamlets of Dhanaulti and Chakrata.

Mussoorie, Queen of the Hills and Dehradun, capital city of the retired, have been popular destinations with both plebs and celebs – the former come to Mussoorie for a cheap honeymoon in the hills, the latter send their offspring to expensive residential schools in Dehradun and

Mussoorie. An overriding factor contributing to their popularity is their proximity to Delhi – it takes but a few hours to exchange urban anarchy for sylvan heights.

TRAIL VIII : DELHI-MUSSOORIE

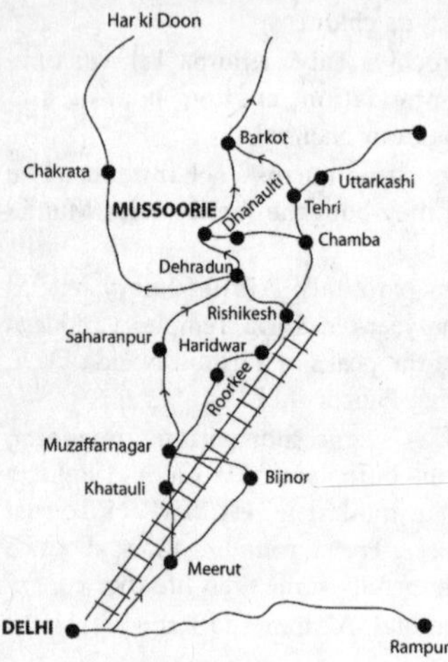

*Map not to scale

The Route: 314 km

Delhi→255 km→Dehradun→ 35 km→Mussoorie→24 km→ Dhanaulti

Trail Time: The equation is ultra simple – 5 hours at 50 kmph along the highway and you are there in Dehradun. Another hour to negotiate the traffic that clogs Dehradun's main thoroughfare and the short distance of 35 km up to Mussoorie, another 24 km to Dhanaulti on the Mussoorie-Chamba road and the journey is over and done with. Chakrata lies on the opposite axis and is as beautiful. So how about it?

Follow the Road

Delhi-Dehradun: 255 km (5-6 hrs)
Dehradun-Chakrata: 98 km(3hrs)
Dehradun-Mussoorie: 35 km (1 hr)
Mussoorie-Dhanaulti: 24 km (1 hr)

Be Different

Catch the early morning superfast, ultra comfortable Shatabdi Express to Dehradun. Hire a cab, rent a car or hop into a bus bound for Mussoorie/ Dhanaulti and leave the pain and the strain of driving to somebody else. Air connections, few though they are, are available to Dehradun's Jolly Grant Airport. The number of bus and coach tours between Delhi, Dehradun and Mussoorie is quite staggering – Uttaranchal Roadways, UP Roadways and DTC operate overnight/day deluxe and ordinary bus services, all of which are available from Inter State Bus Terminal in Delhi.

Stopovers

Head straight for the hills. Hightail your way past small town Uttar

Pradesh, its crowded roads, its overwhelming odours and its nerve-racking traffic to the (relatively) cool tranquility of Dehradun, Mussoorie and Dhanaulti. Allow the family just one stop – tea break, lunch break, loo break, whatever – at Chital, between Khatauli and Muzaffarnagar after 100 km on the clock. Next stop – Dehradun.

Dehradun (640 m): Lying between the rolling Shivalik and towering Himalayan Ranges is a valley that was once infinitely more charming and picturesque than it looks now – and nestling in this valley is a city so old that it dates back to the Vedic era. Dehradun was fêted for its genteel beauty and serene charm before deforestation, development and dampness diminished its attraction. But despite paying a high price for progress – ad hoc growth, overcrowding, chronic water and electricity shortage, endless construction, relentless quarrying and near total devastation of forest cover – diehard fans of Dehradun love it immensely and unequivocally.

Dehradun, the provisional capital of Uttaranchal, has always enjoyed immense popularity – the Gurkhas of Nepal loved it enough to make it the administrative centre from where they controlled their territories in Garhwal, the British found its climate so salubrious and wholesome that they established educational institutions and set up a garrison here and of course, Indians loved it so much that they worked all over India but retired to Dehradun.

As the gateway to Mussoorie and with plenty of schools and civil and military institutions, Dehradun plays host to itinerant populace who require hotels, guesthouses, lodges, Government Rest Houses, cafés and restaurants. In other words, hotel accommodation and eating out is no problem in a city that caters to visitors all year round.

Chakrata (2135 m): If Mussoorie has its little hidden treasure in Dhanaulti, then Chakrata has to be Dehradun's best kept secret. The short drive up to Chakrata goes

What's in a Name?

When Shakespeare wrote, 'What's in a name?' he hadn't a clue. Take Dehradun – one name with very diverse meanings! The oldest story in terms of antiquity says it's named after Devara, a small village in the foothills of the Himalayas where Dronacharya, guru of the Pandavas and the Kauravas of the Mahabharata, had his ashram. Another story doing the rounds from the Middle Ages says this was the dera (encampment) of Guru Ram Rai of the Udasi Sikhs in the dun or doon – the flat land at the base of a mountain range – and so Dera + Dun= Dehradun!

through countryside flush with rich farms and prosperous lychee and mango orchards around the little townships of Prem Nagar, Herbertpur and Vikaspur. The road begins its ascent at Kalsi, a small town with a long hoary history going back to the Mauryan Empire (400 BC).

Chakrata is the centre of Jaunsar Bhabar – home ground of the Jaunsari tribe – a region composed entirely of a succession of steep mountains interspersed with gorges, waterfalls and forests of conifers, rhododendrons and oaks. Chakrata has always been there – waiting to take its rightful place on the tourist circuit – but its enormous potential remains largely underdeveloped. The British established a cantonment here in the 1870s – old British barracks, a cemetery and training school are still there and except for the cemetery, very much in use.

A road, potholed and pitted, connects Chakrata to Mussoorie by way of Goraghati, Lakhamandal and Kuwa (64 km). Kuwa (1090 m) lies on the route to Yamunotri – head north to get there or south for Mussoorie (71 km).

Lost Tribe?

Fair- skinned, light-eyed women with Caucasian features, dressed in long black skirts topped with little black jackets – polyandrous, independent and at par with their menfolk – definitely not your typical Indian woman. But then, there is little stereotypical about the Jaunsari tribe. One of its most unusual and effective socio-cultural features is the practice of 'Chhinga' – a supernatural element used to keep peace between two warring parties.

Chhinga means that while they may not enter each other's house, eat together or share the water source, they will maintain cordial relations and cooperate in community work till such time as one of them accepts it is his fault. That happens when the wrath of the supernatural power falls on the guilty party, showing him the error of his ways! Interestingly, Chhinga may take one year or forever to work but till it does, violence is avoided and social harmony preserved.

Mussoorie (2005 m): Would India have had any hill stations (as opposed to hill settlements) if it were not for the British? A moot point and a question that has no answer because the British developed every promising mountain in their desperation to escape the Indian summer. More to the point – the closest getaway from the scorching summer days of the United Provinces lay in Mussoorie, a classic 1820s hill retreat custom made to pander to colonial British tastes. From Savoy Hotel to Connaught Castle, from Tipperary to Castle Hill, from Shamrock Cottage to Bleak House – Mussoorie was anglicized to create a domain for the diaspora, a bit of Britain to delight every Irish, Scot, Welsh or English heart.

By the middle of the 20th century, Mussoorie had become the preserve of India's elite – the prosperous, the pompous, the gracious and the illustrious (and the obnoxious) built or bought grand mansions and stately homes till the abolition of the Privy Purse and inflation put paid to all such pretensions. Now Mussoorie belongs to the hoi polloi, India's burgeoning middle class trying to catch up with the Joneses.

Anyone who doubts Mussoorie's status as Queen of the Hills should check out the local hotel index – they would find over hundred hotels in categories from luxury resorts, deluxe hotels to mid-budget and budget. Summer or winter, rain or shine, tourists and day-trippers arrive by the car- cab- and coach-load, crowding Mussoorie's popular thoroughfare, Mall Road.

The Mall is most often compared to an artery – quite true except it is an artery so clogged that it is in dire need of a bypass. Traffic on the Mall can stand still for hours, opportune for hawkers and vendors but infuriating for everyone else. Nevertheless, life for most visitors revolves around the Mall with its innumerable shops, budget hotels, restaurants, cafés and dhabas, its cab and bus stands. True blue Mussoorie lies further away – out of reach unless you have a car, a good map and foresight. Charleville, Happy Valley, Cloud End, Benog Hill – places that retain much of the original magic of Mussoorie.

Dhanaulti (2250 m): The perfect honeymoon, the ideal retreat, the quiet holiday, the romantic interlude – those looking for a destination that fits any of the above should try Dhanaulti. Barely 24 km on the road to Chamba but light years away from the bedlam of Mussoorie's Mall in terms of ambience is Dhanaulti, a delightful little hamlet, sleepy, slothful and sylvan tucked away in the midst of deep forests of oaks and conifers, rhododendrons and deodars. Dhanaulti is a woody paradise that is just ideal for long walks up shady slopes or quiet tête-à-têtes amidst grassy glens. The only catch in this paragon of a destination is its limited accommodation – a few tourist guesthouses, the GMVN Tourist Bungalow and the Forest Rest House.

Return Leg

Two roads to and from Dhanaulti – one by way of the trail, via Mussoorie and Dehradun, the other by way of Chamba (31 km). The latter is more scenic, snaking its way through apple country with panoramic views of the River Bhagirathi and the Himalayas. Accommodation in Chamba is available at Forest and PWD Rest Houses or at small hotels in town. Chamba to Delhi is a distance of some 294 km via Narendranagar, Rishikesh, Haridwar, Saharanpur and Muzaffarnagar.

Ghosts that Walk in Mussoorie

Make the most of your holiday in Mussoorie – spot a few spooks, bag a couple of ghouls or scalp some sceptres, just don't fall foul of the phantoms! Check these out for starters!

Five hungry ghosts: Way back in 1857, when the sepoys were mutinying in the plains, an Indian khansama of an English family made his point in Mussoorie. He cooked a fine meal, spiked it with poison and fed it to the family of five. He killed them but didn't quite manage to get rid of them – all five members of this family make a regular appearance at their former home (quite properly known as the Haunted House) calling for the cook to serve them their dinner!

The ghost who swings: This ghost stalks the swings in the playground of one of Mussoorie's prominent residential schools. On dark nights, when the moon is away and the wind is quiet, the swings sway wildly – up and down, round and round!

The headless lady: The headless body of a poor English woman murdered (decapitated?) in her hotel room haunts the corridors looking, one presumes, for the missing head!

The Night Rider: Galloping his way down memory lane is the ghost on horseback – the rider returned to England but left his spirit behind to haunt the back roads of Mussoorie.

ASIDES: SIDE BY SIDE

Dakpathar (790 m, 44 km from Dehradun): Hydroelectric project on the River Yamuna is now being developed as a recreation centre by GMVN. The Asian Barrage, a water sports centre with good accommodation and facilities for swimming, kayaking, sailing, canoeing etc is 11 km away.

Devban (2900 m, 16 km from Chakrata): Panoramic views of the Himalayas from this little Jaunsari village that also boasts a Forest Rest House.

Hanol (1429 m, 186 km from Dehradun): Shiva is worshipped as Lord Mahasu in an unusual pagoda-like temple built in the Huna architectural style in this little village on the banks of the River Tons.

Har ki Doon (3566 m, 165 km from Chakrata): Picture-perfect locale in the Himalayas – on the trekking trail to the Jamdar glacier, confluence of the Rivers Tons, Supin and Rupin.
Kalsi (850 m): Famous for its Ashoka Rock Edict on a quartz rock measuring 10 ft by 8 ft dating back to 450 BC and for its Basmati rice, fresh vegetables and fruits, particularly its giant tomatoes.
Kempty Falls (1524 m, 15 km from Mussoorie): The highest cascade around Mussoorie – charming and well-frequented, at its best after the rains. A Forest Rest House provides overnight accommodation booked through DFO, Mussoorie Division (Tel: 0135-232335).
Lakhamandal (1090 m, 58 km from Chakrata): The Kauravas built the Laksha Griha, a palace for their sworn enemies and cousins, the Pandavas, here in 2000 BC or thereabouts. Since the palace was made entirely of shellac, it was easily set aflame with the intention of finishing the Pandavas in one fell swoop. Things didn't go as per plan and the Pandavas lived to fight the Mahabharata. The burnt ruins can still be seen at Lakhamandal.
Lacchiwala & Doiwala (25 km from Dehradun): Picnic spots in the forested tracts around Dehradun – Forest Rest House provides accommodation here.
Mundali (36 km from Chakrata): Unmetalled road but fabulous ski slopes make up for the rough ride. Book rooms in the Forest Rest House well in time – that's the only place to spend the night at.
Nag Tibba (3048 m, 41 km from Mussoorie): Strenuous trek through pine forests, past mountain streams and charming Garhwali villages to get to this peak. Nearest accommodation is the Forest Rest House at the village of Deolsari, some 5 hours away.
Paonta Sahib (60 km from Dehradun): This Sikh pilgrimage site on the banks of the Yamuna has a beautiful gurudwara dedicated to Guru Gobind Singh. GMVN Tourist Rest House, Irrigation Dept Rest House and private hotels provide ample accommodation.
Rajaji National Park: Semi-deciduous and deciduous forests make up this 820 sq km national park in the Shivaliks.
Sahastradhara (11 km from Dehradun): A thousand streams and a sulphur spring. A pretty and popular picnic spot, waterfall and a limestone cave along the River Baldi.
Surkhanda Devi Temple (35 km from Mussoorie): This temple commemorates the spot where Sati's head fell.
Tyuni (1080 m, 68 km from Chakrata): On the road to Himachal Pradesh and Har ki Doon – a favourite trekking destination.
Yamuna Bridge (30 km from Mussoorie): Anglers' paradise packed with Himalayan trout. Fishing license required and can be obtained from the office of the DFO, Mussoorie Division (Tel: 01362-232335).

TRAIL IX: DELHI-CORBETT NATIONAL PARK

Take an Englishman in an Indian setting, give him a few guns, hire a dozen beaters and let him loose in thousands of acres of a dark, dark jungle busy with tigers, some fond of eating men and others just fond of eating. And you have the makings of a legend and the ingredients for a bestseller. Jim Corbett, the legendary hunter, did write that bestseller (and others too) after despatching countless tigers, man-eating or otherwise, to the tigers' Valhalla. Corbett's domain in Kumaon now houses one of India's major tiger reserves and is named for the great hunter, not because he killed so many of them but because he was the first to read the writing on the wall and thereafter became an ardent advocate of tigers' rights.

To appreciate Jim Corbett's efforts and to see the King of the Jungle in his native habitat, follow this trail to Dhikala in the heart of tiger country.

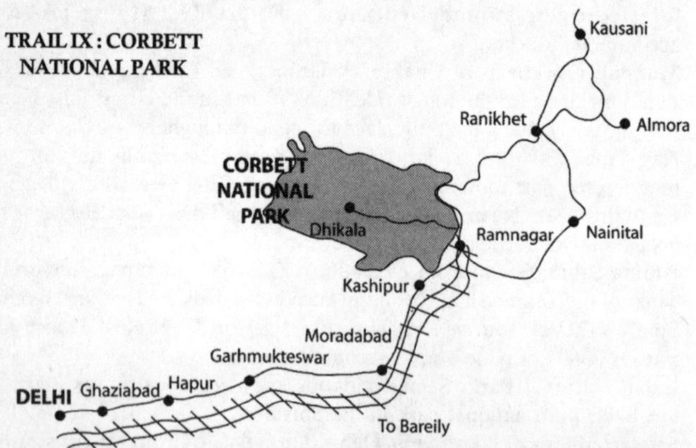

*Map not to scale

The Route: 340 km

Delhi→163 km→Moradabad→97 km→Kashipur→28 km→Ramnagar→51 km→Dhikala

Follow the Road

Delhi-Moradabad: 163 km (3-4 hrs)

Moradabad-Kashipur: 97 km (2-3 hrs)

Kashipur-Ramnagar: 28 km (.5 hr)

Ramnagar-Dhikala: 51 km (1 hr)

Trail Time: 7-8 hours giving due consideration to the traffic that either moves at a murderous pace or is incredibly slow to get going. NH 24 is obviously popular and every driver, whether he drives a bullock cart, a Bolero, Benz or BMW believes he is King of the Road and therefore has the divine right not to give way to the traffic behind.

Stopovers

NH 24 hurries straight down towards Moradabad, but on a bad day that is just about the only thing that moves. Time crawls, most drivers do an impersonation of having nowhere to go and those in a hurry get to taste life in the slow lane. Contributing its bit to this trance-like situation is the all-pervading odour of molasses, treacly, thick and slow to dissipate! But that's on a bad day – now fortunately few and far between because of the Moradabad bypass – a three-leafed clover that has proved truly lucky for vehicular traffic along NH 24.

Grab a bite at Moradabad, refuel and stoke up the fire to tackle the road that lies ahead. Turn left off the national highway to take the road to Kashipur, famed for its unusual yellow chilli peppers and little else. The gas stations on this stretch of the road offer loos – with the sole advantage of privacy. For the rest, the wheat fields flanking the road provide more hygienic albeit open-air loos with no odour! The folks who live in this area are totally fearless – cattle amble across the road, men hold profound conversations, boys on cycles slalom their way between potholes, kids play tag more on than off the road, women put out washing to dry and tent house-owners spread motheaten carpets across the same road, not in welcome but following some perverse logic that believes the carpets will emerge cleaner after dust- and dirt-encrusted tyres have driven over them. So drive cautiously, ready to avoid the unexpected intruder.

Different Strokes

An early morning start is just about the only way to escape Delhi's chaotic traffic, so spring out of that comfortable bed, climb into that car and get going as quickly as you can. Adding impetus to this quick move is the fact that when the world wakes up, truckies sleep. So you miss Delhi's inhouse traffic and you escape the trucks – do you really need any more reasons to get moving?

Take a Train

The nearest railhead is at Ramnagar with convenient train connections to Delhi, Lucknow and Moradabad. Jeeps and buses are available at Ramnagar for the ride to Dhikala.

Ramnagar (300 m): The gateway to Corbett National Park – a must-stop to obtain the permission of the Director, Corbett National Park, without whose sanction entering the Park limits is not possible. So first stop has to perforce be at the Reception Centre, Corbett National Park, Ramnagar (Tel: 05947 – 2853189, 285332). Ramnagar also offers a better class of accommodation – swank resorts and deluxe hotels – than any found in the Park premises.

The Park: Nestling in the foothills of the Himalayas, India's first wildlife sanctuary was established in 1936 after intensive consultation with Jim Corbett (a keen conservationist by this time). In its first avatar, the reserve was the Hailey National Park and was named Corbett much later. The River Ramganga is the lifeline of Corbett Tiger Reserve and its catchment area sustains both flora and fauna. The river creates the Park's richly contoured topography of valleys, ridges and ravines that bequeath a treasure house of natural habitats. The varied landscape nurtures diverse vegetation – pastures of tall grass known as chaurs unroll across the valley floor, dense stands of sal and deciduous forest cloak the hilly ridges, thorny shrubs, bamboo and sheesham cover the ravines through which flow myriad little streams. Living off this mind-boggling environment are a staggering number of animals – 50 kinds of mammals, 580 species of birds and at least 25 varieties of reptiles. The Ramganga River teems with mahseer, gharial and the fearsome Indian crocodile, the mugger. Darters, cormorants, egrets, storks and lapwings and kingfishers stalk the edges of the rivers or sit atop dead trees in wait for the imprudent fish.

Leopard, jungle cat, fishing cat, monkey, langur, barking deer, chital, antelope, sloth bear, Himalayan black bear, Indian wild dog, jackal, yellow-throated marten, Himalayan palm civet, Indian grey mongoose, common otter, porcupine, black-naped hare and elephant are just a preview of the many mammals found in the park.

Park Permit

Overnight visitors to Corbett require an entry permit as well as reserved accommodation in one of the guesthouses. Day visits to Dhikala were banned in 1990 and only those visitors who have confirmed overnight accommodation are permitted to enter from the National Park Gate.

It is a wise man who books bed and board well in time, and so avoids the censure of his friends and family. For bookings, write to Field Director, Project Tiger, Corbett National Park, PO Ramnagar, District Nainital, Uttaranchal – 244715.

Tigers, of course, are the raison d'être of Corbett, which is why Project Tiger (set up with aid from the World Wildlife Fund), aimed at protecting and conserving the highly threatened Indian Tiger, was launched at Dhikala in the Corbett National Park on 1 April 1973.

Project Tiger

Project Tiger was launched at Corbett National Park in 1973 with the sole aim of preserving the rapidly dwindling population of tigers in India. The scheme was later extended to over a dozen reserves all over the country. The efforts of the hundreds of wildlife administrators, wardens, guards and naturalists paid off with the population of Indian tiger stabilizing at 3000, of which 100 are to be found at Corbett.

Dhikala: Dhikala, at the heart of the Park's core area, is perfectly located on a grassy plateau overlooking the Ramganga Reservoir as it curves its way to the main basin. The water hole and the grasslands of the Dhikala Chaur provide the ideal viewing area for wildlife. Tigers are most elusive but herds of deer, the odd wild boar and elephants are commonly sighted.

A range of accommodation is available at Dhikala including Forest Rest Houses, lodges, cabins, huts, dormitories and campsites. Restaurants, a library, a field post office, first aid centre, an open-air theatre and a provision store are some of the other facilities available for visitors. The Forest Rest Houses are ideally located in picturesque spots around the park ideal for wildlife enthusiasts, photographers, anglers, bird watchers – the true lovers of the jungle in its raw natural state.

Homeward Bound

If there is any wanderlust leftover after a sojourn in the heart of tiger country, head for the hills. Kausani,

Wildlife Safaris

Walking is permitted only in some designated areas and then only if accompanied by licensed guides. The best way to travel within the Park is by jeep – these can be rented for the park trips from Ramnagar, from the KMVN Tourist Lodge and other travel agencies and elephant safaris are available at Dhikala, Khinanauli and Bijrani. Elephant rides are conducted every morning and evening in season – November to June. Day visitors are only allowed into some sections and can make the trip on the bus that takes off early mornings from the Project Tiger Office in Ramnagar.

Kumaon's ultra romantic resort, is barely 4 hrs and 160 km away from Ramnagar. Ranikhet is even closer – just under 100 km on the way to Kausani, so pick one or do them both. Kausani showcases the Himalayas to perfection – 350 km of power packed mountains that match their mood to the colours of the Sun God present such a feast for the eyes that even determined diehards like the Mahatma fell victim to their allure. Ranikhet, of course, wears an old world aura that instantly identifies it as a garrison town. Return home to Delhi with the spirits restored after a few days in the splendid hills of Kumaon.

ASIDES: SIDE BY SIDE

Corbett Falls (on the Ramnagar-Kaladhungi road): Campsites in this densely-forested area near the 20 m waterfalls provide a great wilderness experience.

Dhikuli (8 km from Ramnagar): Archaeological ruins add to this place's attractions.

Girija Devi (10 km from Ramnagar): Midstream of River Kosi is a rock on which stands the temple dedicated to Girija Devi – the venue of a huge fair on Kartik Purnima.

Kotabagh (10 km from Ramnagar): Ruins provide an insight into the glorious reign of the powerful Chand dynasty that ruled over much of this area.

Kaladhungi (700 m, 35 km from Ramnagar): The residence of the legendary Jim Corbett is now a museum housing mementoes, relics and archives. A Forest Rest House in the area provides the accommodation.

Lohachaur (15 km from Ramnagar): Angle in the River Kosi for the legendary Mahseer, the big game fish of Indian rivers. Permits to have a go must be obtained from the Project Tiger Office in Ramnagar or check with your resort if they can arrange a fishing expedition.

TRAIL X: DELHI-VALLEY OF FLOWERS & HEMKUND SAHIB

'Here flowerful pastures with clear running streams are set against silver birches and shining snow peaks. Dew lies thick on the flowers, birds sing in the surrounding forest and the air is pure and charged with floral smells.... To me it will remain the "Valley of Flowers" a valley of peace and perfect beauty where the human spirit may find repose.' – Frank S. Smythe, Mountaineer, Explorer and Botanist.

Some of the world's most wondrous treasures have been

TRAIL X : DELHI-VALLEY OF FLOWERS

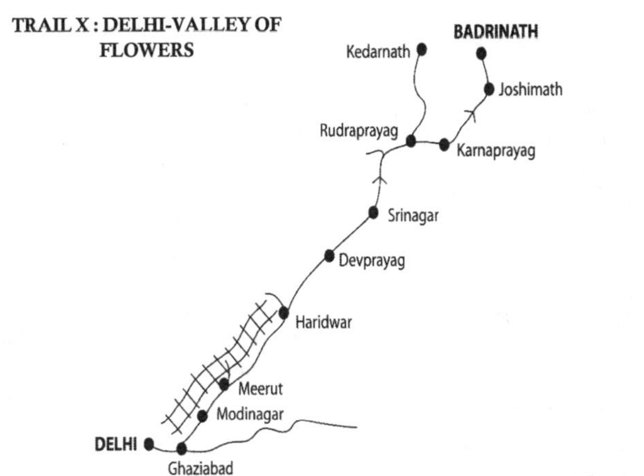

*Map not to scale

discovered by sheer serendipity, pure fluke or a lucky chance. The Valley of Flowers qualifies for top place on that list for it was discovered for no other reason than that Frank Smythe lost his way and instead found an isolated flower-filled valley hidden in the depths of the Garhwal Himalayas, zealously guarded by the very same mountains.

The Route: 528 km

Delhi→228 km→Rishikesh→ 180 km→Karnaprayag→82 km→ Joshimath→20 km→Gobindghat→ 15 km→Ghangaria→3 km→Valley of Flowers

Trail Time: 15 hours, door to door. The last 18 km have to be negotiated on foot and of course, more nimble footwork is required inside the valley. It is a fairly comfortable drive on NH 58 till Saharanpur and then on the state road to Rishikesh and Joshimath.

Follow the Road

Delhi-Rishikesh: 228 km (5-6 hrs)
Rishikesh-Karnaprayag: 180 km (4-5 hrs)
Karnaprayag-Joshimath: 82 km (3 hrs)
Joshimath-Gobindghat: 20 km (1 hr)
Gobindghat-Ghangaria: 15 km (1.5 hr trek)
Ghangaria-Valley of Flowers: 3 km (.5 hr)
Ghangaria-Hemkund Sahib: 6 km (1 hr)

Stopovers

The road from Rishikesh to Joshimath and Gobindghat treads the path taken by countless pilgrims on their way to the holy shrine of Lord Badrinath. The road climbs its way past the Panch Prayags, the five sacred confluences and pilgrim strongholds of Devaprayag, Rudraprayag, Karnaprayag, Nandprayag and Vishnuprayag before arriving at Gobindghat.

Or Try Another Approach

Though there are many trains between Delhi and Haridwar, the best is the superfast Dehradun Shatabdi. Along with the ticket comes the Shatabdi breakfast of wilted omelette, soggy fries and limp toast or greasy cutlets, the same fries and toast that can be washed down with a decent cuppa tea or coffee – decent because you control the milk and sugar. Both buses and taxis are available right outside the station for Joshimath or Gobindghat. GMVN and private tour companies have coach tours to the Valley of Flowers and to Hemkund Sahib.

Gobindghat (1828 m): The ascent to the Valley of Flowers begins from this little settlement on the approach road to Badrinath. Gobindghat is a good place to put down roots (pro tem, only!) as it has decent accommodation including a Forest Rest House. Ponies and guides can be hired at Gobindghat for the laborious trek that lies ahead.

The trail uses the suspension bridge to cross the Alaknanda before heading north along the River Bhuiyndar Ganga towards the villages of Pulna, Bhuiyndar and Ghangaria. Breathlessness becomes a constant companion on this trail – either from the steep gradient or from gasping at the incredibly beautiful vista spread around. The route is punctuated with waterfalls, wild flowers, forests and quaint little hamlets; above stand snow-covered ranges while below stretches the valley like some pretty patchwork quilt. Luckily the track is dotted with little shacks and shops selling hot tea, bottled water and hot snacks, the motivation for a break and a breather.

Ghangaria (3048 m): This is the closest place for an overnight halt, barely 3 km short of the Valley and options include choosing from suites at the Forest Rest House, rooms at the Tourist Rest House and other private guesthouses, tents at the GMVN campsite and at the gurudwara in Ghangaria which provides floor space to everyone irrespective of religious affiliation.

Valley of Flowers (3200 m-6765 m): Ringed by majestic snow-clad peaks that are dazzling in the bright sunlight or moody as the overcast sky, the Valley of Flowers is divided into two by the River Pushpawati, icy cold from its

The Serpent in this Garden of Eden

It is mandatory for every garden to have a serpent in order to qualify as Eden and the Valley meets this requirement. Along the left bank of the River Pushpawati are flat tracts of land, one of them known as Nag Tal – the place of the Serpent King, Nag himself. The flowers and foliage that grow here are toxic and extremely harmful – locals believe the venom of the Snake God lies within these plants and whoever plucks them does so at his own peril.

source in the glaciers of the Rataban and Nilgiri Ranges. Small streams crisscross the valley creating moist little pockets wherein grow an astounding variety of wild flowers. The smaller streams are shallow and easy to wade across, the bigger ones call for a balancing act on log bridges or a speedy zip zap over snow bridges, frozen sections of the river.

A veritable cornucopia of blooms – Anemone, Begonia, Geranium, Marsh Marigold, Primula, Potentilla, Aster, Lilium, Himalayan Blue Poppy, Aconite, Delphinium, Ranunculus, Corydalis, Campanula, Impatiens, Iris, Lobelia, Orchid, Saussurea Obvallatta, Strawberry and Rhododendron, to name just a few, carpet this beautiful valley. There is such a staggering variety of flora, medicinal plants (including the life-saving Sanjivini) and herbs to be found here that visitors literally have to wade through knee-high grass and plants to get anyplace.

The valley is accessible from April onwards when the melting snows hydrate the dormant plants into life; peak bloom time is in the late summer from July to August when the valley literally implodes with flowers and fragrances. Come September and an autumnal mood takes over – leaves turn brown and petals fall away as seed pods ripen, readying themselves for next season's display. Winter casts its snowy white mantle on the valley from early November onwards leaving it to sleep under a blanket of thick snow.

NB: Access to the Valley is limited to day trips only – no camping, sleeping or walking away with the flowers or plants.

Hemkund Sahib (4329 m): A steep climb of 6 km from Ghangaria leads to the Lokpal Lake, better known as Hemkund (Lake of Gold). The area remains frozen for the better part of the year till spring arrives, when the snowy white landscape stands transformed with the rich colours of blue forget-me-nots, yellow wild buttercups, pink and red rhododendron, green lichen, ferns and pine trees.

Legend & Lore

The valley was frequented by sages who found in it the perfect ambience and the solitude to meditate and contemplate on issues that drove them away from more populated places. The locals call it 'Nandan Kanan', the divine Garden of Indra, King of Gods.

The valley's strongest mythological association is with Laxmana, younger brother of Rama who meditated on the banks of the Hemkund Lake and whose life was saved by the 'Sanjivini Buti', a herb found only in this valley. In those days, there were even more species of herbs and plants growing in the valley and unable to identify the correct herb, Hanuman, the Monkey God sent to fetch the herb, solved the problem by taking the entire mountain all the way to the southern tip of the Indian peninsula. Makes you wonder how the mountain found its way back, doesn't it?

The King of the Valley is undoubtedly the Brahmakamal – Saussurea Obvallata – a 6-8 inch graceful creamy lotus-like flower with yellow stamens that grows only in the Greater Himalayas at heights above 3800 m and flowers in August-September. Legend has it that celestial maidens would collect the flowers to offer them to Lords Kedarnath and Badrinath.

The flawless complexion of Draupadi, the beautiful wife of the Pandavas, is also attributed to the smooth and velvety bloom (which doesn't give us the license to pluck this rare flower).

The crystalline waters of the lake, fed by the glaciers that flow down from Hathi Parvat and Saptrishi peaks, reflect the icy snowscape of the seven Himalayan peaks that form a protective cordon around it. A temple and gurudwara stand on the edge of this lake considered sacred by the Hindus and even more so by the Sikhs.

Hemkund is associated with the 10th Sikh guru, Guru Gobind Singh, the founder of the Khalsa Panth, who is believed to have meditated on the banks of this holy lake in an earlier incarnation. Possibly the highest shrine in the world, Hemkund was 're-discovered' in the 1930s by a Sikh soldier who found his way here following references in texts penned by Guru Gobind Singh. The Gurudwara at Hemkund has the capacity to feed and house 5000 pilgrims at one time – the accommodation is basic but the food from the Guru's langar is deliciously warm and sustaining.

Return Journey

Take the track to Gobindghat via Ghangaria, then either head up for Badrinath to pay obeisance to the Lord or travel down to Haridwar via Joshimath, Chamoli, Rudraprayag, Srinagar and Rishikesh.

ASIDES: SIDE BY SIDE

Auli (2750m, 8 km from Joshimath): Ski centre of the Garhwal Himalayas – great slopes as well as good accommodation plus professional instructors.
Badrinath (3096 m, 25 km from Gobindghat): The shrine of the Lord of the mountains, Lord Shiva, is one of the holiest in Hindu India.
Kagbhusand Tal (4525 m): This beautiful tarn at the foot of the triangular Mt Khagbhusand (5830 m) is a 3-4 hour trek from Hemkund. Both mountain and lake get their name from the summit that resembles Garur (eagle) aka Kagbhusand.

For more places in and around this area, see Trail IV.

TRAIL XI: CHAR DHAM

The one journey every devout Hindu aspires to undertake in his lifetime is the Char Dham Yatra – the most auspicious and holy of pilgrimages. While it means a lot to have paid obeisance to Lords Badrinath and Kedarnath and the Goddesses Gangotri and Yamunotri individually, it doesn't even compare to the brownie points

TRAIL XI : CHAR DHAM YATRA

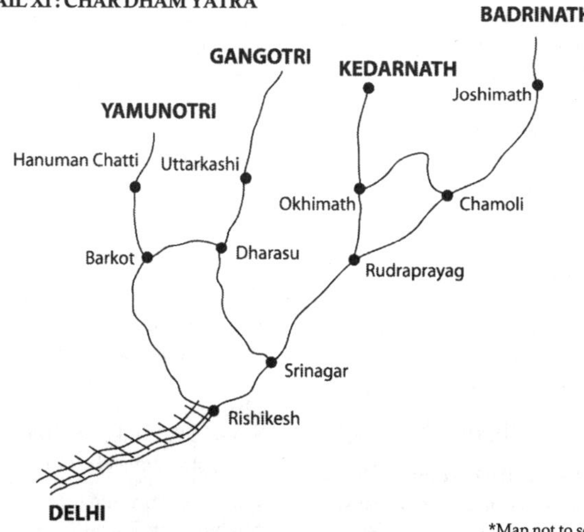

*Map not to scale

scored by doing all four dhams in one go.

The Char Dham Yatra has great religious significance and has been prescribed by Hindu scriptures as the shortest and straightest route to moksha (apart from living a virtuous life, of course!). The four dhams, Yamunotri, Gangotri, Kedarnath and Badrinath, are fairly close to each other but only as the crow flies. Separating them are impregnable mountain ranges and enormous glaciers that make it mandatory to travel up and down, round and around before they can be accessed.

The Route: Char Dham Yatra (1825 km)

Delhi→228 km→Rishikesh→ 222 km→Yamunotri→183 km→ Uttarkashi→96 km→Gangotri→ 165 km→Tehri→171 km→ Kedarnath→51 km→Ohkimath→ 81 km→Chamoli→51 km→ Joshimath→44 km→Badrinath→ 330 km→Haridwar→203 km→ Delhi

Trail Time: Nearly 60 hours of driving lie ahead – we did say this was one marathon drive. Set aside 7-8 days for Char Dhams but break it up in manageable sections – do a dham at a time, spend the night in comfort and take your time – after all this is the yatra of a lifetime.

Stopovers

The road to Rishikesh: We're on the road to Rishikesh, the first stop on the trail to Char Dham that

Follow the Road

Delhi-Rishikesh: 228 km (5-6 hrs)
Rishikesh-Yamunotri: 222 km (5-6 hrs)
Yamunotri-Uttarkashi: 183 km (6-7 hrs)
Uttarkashi-Gangotri: 96 km (4 hrs)
Gangotri-Tehri: 165 km (6-7 hrs)
Tehri-Kedarnath: 171 km (7-8 hrs)
Kedarnath-Okhimath: 53 km (1.5 hrs)
Okhimath-Chamoli: 81 km (3 hrs)
Chamoli-Joshimath: 51 km (2 hrs)
Joshimath-Badrinath: 44 km (1.5 hrs)
Badrinath-Haridwar: 330 km (10-11 hrs)
Haridwar-Delhi: 203 km (5 hrs)

All the Way

This is one marathon journey, to be undertaken only after much thought and adequate planning, especially if you are your own chauffeur. Plan on covering manageable segments per day, organize the overnight halts so as to arrive at the temples by mid-day at the latest – and set aside a sizeable number of hours for the darshans. Avoid driving after dark – these mountain roads are definitely not geared for night hauls so don't be in a tearing hurry to reach any place. Neither the dhams nor the temples are going anywhere, so take your time, drive safely and sensibly.

Bus companies and tour operators run bus tours for the Char Dhams that are organized so as to cover the four places in the shortest time span. Alternately, hire a comfortable MUV (Qualis, Sumo or Versa) with a savvy driver and then sit back to enjoy the yatra. GMVN also offers coach and car tours of the Char Dhams.

inspired John Lennon to burst into song – 'On the road to Rishikesh... Underneath the mountain ranges/ Where the wind that never changes/Touched the windows of my soul!'

Leaving Delhi behind is never a hardship for those who live and work here, especially when ahead lies Kedarkhand, the fabled land of the gods. The road to Rishikesh takes the NH 58 till Muzaffarnagar and then bifurcates onto the taxing, pitted and pot-holed state road to Haridwar via the university town of Roorkee. Follow the road and the River Ganga to reach Rishikesh.

Rishikesh (340 m): Not so far in miles but extremely distant from the hurly-burly and hustle-bustle of Delhi is Rishikesh, an ancient spiritual and religious centre on the banks of the Ganga. It is believed that it was here in the wilderness that Rishi Raibhya did such severe penance and for so long that Lord Vishnu appeared before him as Hrishikesh (One who controls the senses) and thus blessed, this place came to be known as Rishikesh. Over the years Rishikesh has evolved into the spiritual capital of yoga with innumerable ashrams that offer classes and courses.

Rishikesh's Triveni Ghat is possibly the most visited and naturally the most crowded place where the hordes come to offer prayers to the river and cleanse themselves of past and present misdeeds with a holy dip in its sacred waters. A little ahead stands the surreal Laxmana Jhoola, a suspension bridge across the river where once swung a rope bridge used by Laxmana, brother of Rama.

Accommodation is no problem in Rishikesh – ashrams and dharamshalas abound and provide spartan and reasonably priced rooms. The only catch is that residents have to abide by their pretty stringent rules.

As per the scriptures, the Char Dham Yatra should be undertaken from east to west, so first port of call is at Yamunotri, the source of the holy Yamuna.

Yamunotri (3185 m): When the River Ganga descended from her celestial abode, she came with such force that the earth and all living beings were in danger of being washed away. Which obviously would have defeated the purpose of her earthly visit! So Shiva came to the rescue, trapped the river in his matted locks and released it in slow motion, in small controllable streams and the River Yamuna was one of them.

Next to the 19th century temple commissioned by the Maharani of

Jaipur to commemorate Yamuna's first appearance are thermal springs so hot that devotees cook rice and potatoes before offering it to the deity. Behind the temple, plummeting down from heights of 2000 m plus, is a magnificent waterfall made up of the melting waters of the Banderpoonch Glacier, the bonafide source of the Yamuna.

Short of Yamunotri are the pilgrim towns called chattis – places where pilgrims sleep over, stock up, muster resources and hire mules or manpower for the final assault– Hanuman Chatti and Janki Chatti – are two of the biggest chattis with abundant albeit basic facilities for pilgrims.

Gangotri (3048 m): Like a roller coaster that goes up, down and up, the trail descends to Barkot (43 km from Hanuman Chatti), then to Dharasu Bend (58 km) before beginning its ascent towards Uttarkashi on its way to Gangotri, the sacred source of the Ganga. Uttarkashi, a small town on the banks of the Bhagirathi, encircled by Rivers Varuna and Assi, houses innumerable temples, monuments, ashrams and the Nehru Institute of Mountaineering. Fast developing as the adventure capital of Uttaranchal, Uttarkashi is a good place for a break in the journey, especially because it is used to handling tourist and pilgrim traffic and has decent hotels, cafés and dhabas.

The last 100 km stage before Gangotri should be done in daylight as the road is usually crowded with trucks carrying potatoes – the famous 'Pahari Aloo' – or pilgrims! The motorable road passes vertically-built villages, pine- clad hills and sharp-edged cliffs and travels all the way to the shrine. But before it can do so, it has to negotiate the awesome Bhagirathi Ravine, which looks as if the combined might of the Rivers Bhagirathi Ganga and Jadh Ganga have riven a cleft in the mountain. Gaumukh, the cow's mouth shaped opening at the foot of the Gangotri glacier, is the true source of the river.

Garhwal Mandal Vikas Nigam, the authority responsible for the development of the region, runs Tourist Rest Houses at Harsil, Lanka, Bhaironghati and Gangotri. Guesthouses, dharamshalas and lodges are also available in plenty, so accommodation is never a problem, so long as one is willing to accept basic bed and board facilities.

Kedarnath (3584 m): To go to Kedarnath, take the road down from Gangotri, past Uttarkashi to Tehri, then another 55 km to Srinagar, the former capital of the kingdom of Tehri Garhwal. Ahead lies Rudraprayag, sanctified and glorified as the confluence of the twin streams of the Ganga – the Mandakini coming down from the direction of Kedarnath and Alaknanda from Badrinath. From Rudraprayag, the road to

Kedarnath crosses the Alaknanda, passes through a tunnel and then goes along the banks of the River Mandakini past Tilwara, Chandrapuri, Okhimath, Guptakashi, Sonprayag till it terminates at Gaurikund. The stretch of road between Guptakashi and Gaurikund is partially metalled and narrow, so the flow of traffic is regulated and restricted by a gate system that allows only one stream of traffic at a time. While the wait for a turn to go up or down can be quite frustrating, it does ensure that there are no headlamp-to-headlight confrontations. The last leg consists of a 14 km trek/walk, pony or piggyback ride to Kedarnath.

The shrine at Kedarnath is highly venerated as one of the 12 Jyotirlingas of Lord Shiva. Lord Shiva, embodiment of all passions, the most powerful god in the Hindu Pantheon, the one blessed with the awesome power to unleash cosmic devastation and destruction, is worshipped in many different forms. At Kedarnath, he is enshrined as the hump of the bull he metamorphosed himself into to escape the guilt-racked, extremely penitent Pandavas. Shiva led the Pandavas a fine dance across the Garhwal Himalayas and just as Bhima, the Pandava strongman, thought he had caught the bull by the hump, Shiva disappeared into the ground, leaving poor Bhima holding nothing but the hump.

Jai Bhole Shankar – the God Who is Forever Doped

In their collective wisdom, the many gods of the Hindu Pantheon decided that the only way to contain the destructive might of Shiva was to keep him permanently doped out! So on Maha Shivaratri, the night Shiva performs his Cosmic Dance of Death and Destruction, the God is offered opium, cannabis and marijuana and the Maha Shivaratri special prasad consists of thandai, a potent intoxicating drink made from cannabis, almonds, and milk.

Badrinath (3096 m): One of the most scenic drives in all of Garhwal is on the road connecting Okhimath to Chamoli via the district headquarters at Gopeshwar. The panoramic splendour of the Himalayas defies description – no adjectives can accurately describe the Himalayas as seen from Chopta, magnificent in scale and resplendent with the colours – snow white, red gold, pale pink, crimson or purple – that they absorb from the sun as it completes its east-west circuit.

Vishnu, one of the three gods of the Hindu Trinity, went underground in these very mountains in his quest for the less worldly, more detached lifestyle considered appropriate for gods by the Sage Narada. When his consort Parvati finally caught up with him and begged him to return to the delights of domesticity, the God decreed that henceforth this region would be 'Tapobhumi', the land of meditation and penance. And true to his directive, this part of the Himalayas became the happy hunting grounds for ascetics, hermits, mendicants, sages and sadhus.

Lord Badri resides at his temple in Badrinath cradled by the snow-capped peaks of the twin ranges of Nar and Narayan and watched over by the awesome Mt Neelkantha. The shrine is closed during the winter months (November to May) when Lord Badri moves to his winter residence in the Narsimha Temple in Joshimath.

Return Leg

The ride home always takes less time, or certainly seems to! But Badrinath to Delhi is a pretty long journey – all 533 km of it, and while it can be done in a day, a break at Haridwar makes it infinitely less taxing. Plan an early morning take-off from Badrinath with a layover at Haridwar and then reward yourself with short stops at the Panch Prayags – the five holy confluences of the Bhagirathi Ganga and her siblings, the Rivers Alaknanda, Mandakini, Dhauli Ganga and Pindar. The big five – Vishnuprayag, Nandaprayag, Karnaprayag, Rudraprayag and Devaprayag – lie on the road from Badrinath to Haridwar and are revered as holy confluences. That they are visually very exciting is an added bonus.

TREKKING IN KUMAON & GARHWAL

Wandering mendicants, sadhus, sages and swamis were the very first trekkers to walk this hallowed land. Then came a steady stream of pilgrims looking for moksha or in search of God but more often than not ending up dead – so uncharted was the territory, so treacherous the terrain, so wild the weather and so hungry the beasts that stalked the dense tracts of forests that then covered the mountain sides.

The modern trekker has the advantage of arriving in terrain that has been well walked and well surveyed – maps detail the smallest stream, the deepest chasm, the highest mountain pass and the most distant settlement. Specialized agencies lead the way armed with global positioning systems, walkie-talkies, radio sets and whatnots making trekking safer than a walk around the neighbourhood. But, and this is big but – no amount of high tech equipment and expertise can anticipate nature's whims and idiosyncrasies and that's what makes trekking so exciting and addictive an activity.

For those bitten by the trekking bug, Kumaon and Garhwal offer a host of prospects ranging from extremely exacting mountain trekking to softer options in the lower hills and plains of Uttaranchal. Uttaranchal's boundaries begin in the fertile farmlands and dense jungles of the Terai –Bhabar belt before ascending to altitudes above 7000 m, in between providing the perfect terrain for all manners of adventure sports, especially trekking. The landscape is quite awesome in scale and scope, metamorphosing from lush farmlands and deciduous jungles in the lower altitudes to terraced fields, conifer forests, mountain tarns, swift rivers, alpine meadows and magnificent peaks in the higher elevations.

Because of the vastness of the terrain and altitude variations, treks can be undertaken the whole year round. Treks range from low altitude treks in winter to the crossing of high passes in summer when the snowline recedes. The two best seasons (also the safest) for trekking beyond 4500 m are mid-April to May-June before the monsoon and September-November (post monsoons); winter trekking is possible between November and March in altitudes below 2500 m.

Permits

Indian nationals need not take permission for trekking in any area outside the Inner Line. For routes inside the Inner Line, the local District Magistrate's permission or that of the Central Home Ministry is necessary and should be taken prior to departure.

Foreigners cannot cross the Inner Line but can trek to altitudes up to 4900 m on tourist visas. Treks above 4900 m are to be undertaken only with prior permission from the Indian Mountaineering Foundation, provided no peak is attempted. Camera permits are also necessary and can be obtained from the IMF. For more information, permits etc contact or write to Secretary, Indian Mountaineering Foundation, Benito Juarez Road, Anand Niketan, New Delhi – 110021 (Tel: 011-22671211, Fax: 011-26883412).

Kumaon

Kumaon can be divided into three trekking regions: the foothills of the Himalaya (Nainital and Champawat districts), the hill areas of Almora, Ranikhet, Kausani, Chaukori, and Pithoragarh and the Himalayan glacial region beyond Pithoragarh, Bageshwar, Munsiyari and Chaukori.

The lake district of Nainital (Bhim Tal, Sat Tal, Naukuchiya Tal, Khurpa Tal) could well be tailor-made for amateurs and youngsters – the treks in this extremely scenic region are of short duration (including day walks), relatively easy to do and do not involve very much climbing. And transportation is available should the spirits flag and the body tire! Seasoned and experienced trekkers looking for more exacting treks will find them in and around Almora, Ranikhet, Kausani, Chaukori and Pithoragarh. The toughest treks with the highest levels of difficulty are the ones that go to the Himalayan glaciers and high-altitude meadows.

The ideal time for trekking in Kumaon is between May and October/November. Bageshwar, Munsiyari, Pithoragarh, Gwaldam and Chaukori are popular base camps for treks bound for the upper reaches of Kumaon, particularly to the bugyals, snowfields and glaciers of the region.

Trekking Trails

Given here are some trekking routes – the possibilities are endless and since trekking is not a science like mountaineering, a hike from one place to another qualifies as a trek. Before embarking on a venture into Kumaon's wilderness, contact the KMVN Office for maps, advice and reliable guides and porters.

Short Treks: 1-2 day durations

Nainital-Bhimtal: 22 km
Nainital-Sat Tal: 24 km
Nainital-Naukuchiya Tal: 26 km
Almora-Sitlakhet: 37 km
Almora-Binsar: 28 km
Almora-Jageshwar: 34 km
Ranikhet-Chaubatia: 8 km
Kausani-Baijnath: 19 km
Tanakpur-Purnagiri: 19 km
Bageshwar-Kapkote: 24 km

Bageshwar-Pindari Glacier

Altitude: 4625 m ASL
Difficulty Level: High
Distance: 77 km
Route: Song, Dhakuri, Khati, Dwali, Phurkia, Pindari
Time: 3-4 days
Attractions: Temples at Bageshwar, Himalayan Ranges, Pindar River, Pindari Glacier, Nanda Devi Sanctuary (outer limits), Himalayan flora and fauna
Accommodation: Hotels, Forest and PWD Rest Houses

Bageshwar-Kafni Glacier

Altitude: 3840 m ASL
Difficulty Level: Medium to High
Distance: 85 km
Route: Song, Dhakuri, Khati, Dwali, Kafni
Time: 3-4 days
Attractions: Temples at Bageshwar, Himalayan Ranges, Kafni Glacier, Nandakot Peak, Himalayan flora and fauna
Accommodation: Hotels, Forest and PWD Rest Houses and high-altitude tents beyond Dwali

Bageshwar-Sunderdhunga Glacier

Altitude: 6053 m ASL
Difficulty Level: High
Distance: 81 km
Route: Song, Dhakuri, Khati, Jatoli,

Sunderdhunga
Time: 4-6 days
Attractions: Temples at Bageshwar, Himalayan Ranges, Sunderdhunga River, Sunderdhunga Glacier, Himalayan flora and fauna
Accommodation: Hotels, Forest and PWD Rest Houses and campsite at Sunderdhunga

Bageshwar-Namik Glacier

Altitude: 2290 m ASL
Difficulty Level: Medium
Distance: 94 km (50 km by road to Lilti)
Route: Lilti, Gogina, Dhaldhauk, Sutam Khan Pass, Jogi Udiyar to Namik Glacier
(Plan the return trek via Munsiyari)
Time: 3-4 days
Attractions: Temples at Bageshwar, Himalayan Ranges, Namik Glacier, Ramganga and Goriganga Rivers, Himalayan flora and fauna
Accommodation: Hotels, Forest and PWD Rest Houses and high-altitude tents

Munsiyari-Milam Glacier

Altitude: 4242 m ASL
Difficulty Level: High
Distance: 58 km
Route: Lilam, Bog Udiyar, Rilkot, Burphu, Milam village, Milam Glacier
Time: 5-6 days
Attractions: Himalayan panorama at Munsiyari, Himalayan Ranges, Goriganga River, Johar Valley, Suraj Kund, Himalayan flora and fauna, alpine meadows, orchards and high altitude potato farms
Accommodation: Hotels (Munsiyari), Forest and PWD Rest Houses (Milam village) and high-altitude tents

Pithoragarh-Lipu Pass

Altitude: 5334 m ASL
Difficulty Level: High
Distance: 77 km (145 km by road to Pangu via Dharchula)
Route: Pangu, Sirkha, Jipti, Malpa, Budhi, Kalapani, Navidhang
Time: 5-6 days
Attractions: Himalayan panorama, Himalayan Ranges, Kaliganga River, Kali Valley, Himalayan flora and fauna
Accommodation: Hotels, Forest and PWD Rest Houses and high-altitude tents

Garhwal

The Char Dhams – Yamunotri, Gangotri, Kedarnath and Badrinath – are the most frequented trekking routes in Garhwal and generations of devout Hindus have walked their way to nirvana along these trails.

More rugged than Kumaon and infinitely more challenging, Garhwal has some of the highest mountains in the world. It is criss-crossed by innumerable streams and mountain torrents that have scarred deep gorges and ravines into its craggy landscape. The visual appeal of powerful rivers tumbling down

Kumaon Contacts

- Manager, Kumaon Mandal Vikas Nigam, 102 Indraprakash Building, 21 Barakhamba Road, New Delhi Tel: 011-23712246, 23319835 Fax: 011-23327713
- Manager (Trekking), KMVN Tourist Bungalow, Bageshwar
- Tourism Development Officer, KMVN Tourist Bungalow, Kausani
- Divisional Manager (Tourism), KMVN, Secretariat Building, Nainital

mountainsides and the awesome presence of towering mountains combines to pose a challenge that few enthusiasts can resist. So Garhwal is a happy hunting ground for mountaineers, river rafters and trekkers looking to notch another victory in the perpetual battle between man and the elements.

The best season for trekking in Garhwal hills is between May and October. Garhwal's choicest trekking regions are found around the districts of Uttarkashi, Tehri-Garhwal, Pauri-Garhwal, Dehradun and Chamoli.

Trekking Trails

The fun part of trekking is its unstructured, open plan rule – any way which one walks becomes a trekking trail. Garhwal has as many trekking routes as it has towns, villages, lakes, mountains and bugyals – so given below is a preview to a few of them. The list is truly endless and depends on where the trekker is heading. The GMVN organizes a number of treks all year round and also has a roster of approved guides and porters available at Mussoorie, Joshimath and Uttarkashi.

Short Treks: 1-2 day durations

Shivpuri-Pangi Devi: 20 km
Mussoorie-Dhanaulti: 24 km
Mussoorie-Kempty Falls: 12 km
Chakrata-Deoband: 10 km
Dhanaulti-Sahastradhara: 25 km
Bhatwari-Dyara Bugyal: 16 km
Uttarkashi-Nachiketa Tal: 32 km
Uttarkashi-Dodi Tal: 34 km

Dehradun-Har ki Doon

Altitude: 3566 m ASL
Difficulty Level: Medium
Distance: 44 km (By road to Netwar-155 km)
Route: Saur, Taluka, Osla, Har ki Doon
Time: 5-6 days
Attractions: Himalayan panorama, Himalayan Ranges, Himalayan flora and fauna, temples, villages
Accommodation: Forest Rest Houses and high-altitude tents

Mussoorie-Nag Tibba

Altitude: 3048m ASL
Difficulty Level: Medium
Distance: 49 km (excluding 22 km to Dhanaulti by road)

Route: Morina Dhar, Ghodiappa, Nag Tibba
Time: 5-6 days
Attractions: Himalayan panorama, Swargarohini and Nanda Devi Ranges, Himalayan flora and fauna
Accommodation: Forest Rest Houses and high altitude tents

Kalsi-Lakhamandal

Altitude: 2310 m ASL
Difficulty Level: Medium
Distance: 63 km
Route: Baratkhol, Magti, Dungyara, Barontha and Lakhamandal
Time: 4-5 days
Attractions: History and mythology abounds in the Jaunsar Bhabar tribal region. Quaint Jaunsari villages, virgin tracts of conifer and deodar forests, a wealth of Himalayan flora and fauna and splendid scenery
Accommodation: Forest Rest Houses

Kedarnath-Vasuki Tal

Altitude: 3584 m ASL
Difficulty Level: Medium
Distance: 20 km
Route: Gaurikund, Rambara, Garur Chatti, Kedarnath, Vasuki Tal
Time: 2 days
Attractions: Kedarnath shrine, alpine lake, Mandakini River, Mandakini Valley and Chaukhamba peaks
Accommodation: Forest Rest House, GMVN Tourist Bungalow and dharamshalas

Valley of Flowers-Hemkund Sahib

Altitude: 4329 m ASL
Difficulty Level: Medium
Distance: 20-25 km
Route: Gobindghat, Bhuindar, Ghangariya
Time: 2-3 days
Attractions: A cornucopia of Himalayan flora in the Valley of Flowers plus Himalayan panorama and shrine and alpine lake at Hemkund
Accommodation: Forest Rest Houses, GMVN Tourist Rest House and gurudwara at Hemkund

Tehri-Panwali Bugyal

Altitude: 3963 m ASL
Difficulty Level: Medium
Distance: 76 km
Route: Ghansyali, Ghuttu, Gawanchatti, Gaumanda, Duphanda, Panwali
Time: 5-6 days
Attractions: Alpine meadows and pastureland carpeted with wildflowers set against sparkling white snow-clad mountains
Accommodation: Forest Rest Houses

Khatling Glacier

Altitude: 3717 m ASL
Difficulty Level: Medium
Distance: 72 km
Route: Ghuttu, Reeh, Gangi, Kalyani, Biroda, Kharsali, Pachari, Naumuthi, Bhelbagi, Bhumka, Tamakund, Khatling
Time: 6-8 days
Attractions: Hanging glaciers at Ratangian, Jogin and Phating, alpine lakes, Bhilganga River and river valley

Accommodation: Forest Rest Houses, caves, campsites and high altitude tents

Mundoli-Bedni Bugyal

Altitude: 3354 m ASL
Difficulty Level: Medium
Distance: 36 km
Route: Lahjung Pass, Didana, Ali Bugyal, Bedni Bugyal
Time: 6-8 days
Attractions: Alpine meadows, high-altitude mountain passes, Nanda Devi Range, Mt Trishul and mountain tarns
Accommodation: Forest and PWD Rest House, campsites and high-altitude tents

Garhwal Contacts

- Mountaineering Division, Garhwal Mandal Vikas Nigam, Kailash Gate, Muni ki Reti, Rishikesh. Tel: 0135-431793, 432648 Fax: 0135-430372
- The PRO, GMVN, 102 Indraprakash Building, Barakhamba Road, New Delhi –110 001 Tel: 011-23350481, 23327713 Fax: 011-23327713
- Email: info@garhwalhimalayas.com
- General Manager (Tourism) GMVN, 74/1 MG Road, Dehradun – 248001 Tel: 0135-2653817, 2654408 Fax: 0135-2654408
- Regional Tourist Officer, 45 Gandhi Road, Dehradun Tel: 0135-2653217
- Nehru Institute of Mountaineering, Uttarkashi, PO & District Uttarkashi, Garhwal, Uttaranchal

TREKKING TIPS

The easiest way to go on a trek or safari is through a travel agency that will make travel arrangements and organize routes, maps, camping gear, porters, provisions, medical assistance etc. Choose a specialist agency that has expertize, experience and knowledge of the area.

Never go alone – trek in small groups so there is a backup in case of accidents. Let someone know your intended itinerary and when to expect you back.

Befriend the environment: The environment in the mountains is ecologically very fragile and non-biodegradable garbage can cause irreversible damage to it. So read the checklist provided by the IMF and abide by their instructions. Bring back your thrash but not any of the native flora.

Acclimatize: Before embarking on high-altitude treks, first acclimatize to the rarefied air of the mountains.

Know your limitations: Do not attempt to do more than you are capable of – walk moderate distances and stop if you tire or are breathless. Take frequent breaks – feed on high energy snacks and keep up the fluid levels – mountains can be as dehydrating as deserts. Stay away from berries or fruits you cannot identify.

Pace yourself: Avoid high-altitude sickness with a controlled, slow and steady ascent. Climb only 300 m per day at altitudes over 3000 m and a maximum of 400 m over 4000 m.

Dress Right: Buy the best – sturdy footwear with proper ankle support and good traction, a rain cape that can go around and under, a good quality sleeping bag and clothing as specified by the trek operator. Wear two pairs of socks to allow sweat absorption, so buy shoes that can accommodate both pairs.

Medical Cover: Get a thorough medical check-up before embarking on a strenuous trek and carry a well-equipped first aid kit. A certain fitness level is required for high-altitude trekking – make sure you have it.

HOTELS IN UTTARANCHAL

Garhwal: For accommodation and reservations in Government Rest Houses (PWD, Forest and Irrigation), write to:

General Manager (Tourist)
Garhwal Mandal Vikas Nigam Ltd
Survey Chowk
Dehradun-248001.
Tel: 0135-2653817

Assistant General Manager (Tourist)
Garhwal Mandal Vikas Nigam Ltd
Rishikesh-249201
Tel: 01364-31793, 2371783

Deputy Conservator,
Nanda Devi National Park,
Joshimath.

DM Chamoli
Tel: 01372-252192

DFO Badrinath Forest Division

DFO, Mussoorie Division
Tel: 01362-232335

Kumaon: For accommodation and reservations in Government Rest Houses (PWD, Forest and Irrigation), write to:

Kumaon Mandal Vikas Nigam
Central Reservation Centre

Sukhtal, Mallital
Nainital, Uttaranchal
Tel: 05942-236356,231435
Fax: 05942-236374.

Almora

Circuit House
Tel: 05962-230292

Forest Rest House
Tel: 05962-30065

PWD Inspection House
Tel: 05962-230033

Zila Panchayat Dak Bungalow
Tel: 05962-230028

Holiday Home, Almora
Tel: 05962-230250

Tourist Rest House, Jageshwar
Tel: 05962-263028

Tourist Rest House, Nanda Devi, Binsar
Tel: 05962-280176

Tourist Rest House, Sitla
Tel: 05966-244005

Bageshwar

TRH Bagnath
Tel: 05963-222034

Hotel Siddharth
Tel: 05963-222114

Hotel Rajdoot
Tel: 05963-222146

Hotel Annapurna
Tel: 05963-222109

PWD Inspection Bungalow

Zila Panchayat Dak Bungalow

Tourist Reception Centre,
Kumaon Mandal Vikas Nigam

Forest Rest House

Champawat

KMVN Tourist Rest House
Tel: 05965-228630

Hotel Tourist Resort
Tel: 05965-222266

Kurmanchal Hotel
Tel: 05965-222084

PWD Rest House

Forest Rest House

Hotel Mt View
Tel: 05965-22220, 222120

Dehradun

Hotel Ambassador,
Windlers Shopping Complex,
11A Rajpur Road
Dehradun
Tel: 0135-2655831-2,
Fax: 0135-2655830

Hotel Madhuban
97 Rajpur Road
Dehradun
Tel: 0135-2746041, 2749990-4,
Fax: 0135-2746496

Hotel Rang Mahal
43 Gandhi Nagar
Dehradun
Tel: 0135-2655924

Hotel Ajanta Continental
10 Rajpur Road
Dehradun
Tel: 0135-2749595-96-97

Hotel Nivesh (P) Ltd
Mahendra Bihar
Chakrata Road, Dehradun
Tel: 0135-2654970 & 2658901

Hotel Meedo
71 MG Road
Dehradun
Tel: 0135-2657088

Hotel Himshri
17 Rajpur Road
Dehradun
Tel: 0135-2652583, 2653880

Hotel Hilton
54 Haridwar Road
Dehradun
Tel: 0135-2629591, 26629592
Fax: 2622359

Hotel Great Value
74-C Rajpur Road
Dehradun
Tel: 0135-2746094, 2744763
Fax: 2746058

Osho-Resorts
111 Rajpur Road
Dehradun
Tel: 0135-2749544, 2748535

Krishna Hotel
MG Road
Dehradun
Tel: 0135-2629630, 2725487

Hotel Deep Shikha
57/1 Rajpur Road
Dehradun
Tel: 0135-2659888
Fax: 2710990

Hotel Indralok
29 Rajpur Road
Arikant Palace
Dehradun
Tel: 0135-2658143, 2652744

Hotel Kwality
19-B Rajpur Road
Dehradun
Tel:0135-2657230, 2667001, 2657002

Hotel Lalit Palace
38 Krishnanagar
Dehradun
Tel: 0135-2755313, 2755307
Fax: 2755313

Hotel Mecdo's Grand
28 Rajpur Road
Dehradun
Tel: 0135-2743692, 2747171-72, 2743691
Fax: 2745722

Hotel President
6 Astley Hall
Dehradun
Tel: 0135-2657082, 2655783
Fax: 2658883

Hotel Surabhi Palace
Chakrata Road
Dehradun
Tel: 0135-2624970,
Fax: 0135-2628901

Hotel Nanda Tel
113/2 Rajpur Road
Dehradun
Tel: 0135-2747976, 2742654, 2743528

Hotel Atithi
Tyagi Road
Dehradun
Tel: 0135-2627246
Fax: 2629033

Dharchula

Yash Hotel
Bus Station
Tel: 05967-222218

Ganesh Tourist Lodge
Tel: 22130

PWD Rest House

Dhikala-Corbett National Park

For reservations in accommodation inside the Park, contact:

Director,
Corbett Tiger Reserve
Ramnagar-244715
Tel: 05947-251489
Fax: 05947-251376

Dhanaulti

Hotel Chanderlok
Tel: 098370-250167

Hotel Dhanaulti Crown Plaza
Tel: 0-250167

Hotel Drive In

Maple Orchard Resort

Satkar Guest House

Joshimath

Anand Hotel
Tel: 01389-222343, 222264

Hotel Dronagiri
Tel: 01389-222254
Fax: 222221

Hotel Kamet
Tel: 01389-222155

Hotel Uday Palace
Tel: 01389-222004

Hotel Shivlok
Tel: 01389-222050

Kausani

Hotel Sagar
Tel: 05962-245018
Fax: 245338

Hotel Himalaya
Tel: 05962-245039

Hotel Uttarakhand
Tel: 05962-245012

Hotel Krishna Mount View
Tel/Fax: 05962-245008, 245022

Hotel Prashant
Tel: 05962-245037, 245270

Hotel Sun and Snow Inn
Tel: 05962-245010

Tourist Bungalow
Kumaon Mandal Vikas Nigam
Tel: 05962-245006

Zila Panchayat Dak Bungalow

Forest Rest House

State Bungalow

Anasakti Ashram

Hotel Shakti

Hotel Neelkanth

Lohaghat

Tourist Rest House
Mayawati
Tel: 059653-234313

Hotel Greater Kailash
Tel: 059653-23178

Hotel Deep
Tel: 059653-23063

Amar Jyoti Hotel

PWD Inspection House.

Mussoorie

Jaypee Residency Manor
Barlowganj
Mussoorie-248 122
Tel: 0135-2631800
Fax:0135-2631022

Savoy
The Mall
Mussoorie-248179
Tel: 0135-2631819
Fax: 0135-2631023

Ambica Resorts Pvt Ltd
The Mall Library
Mussoorie-248179
Tel: 0135-2632160, 2633548

Hotel Filigree
Camel's Back Road, Kulri
Mussoorie-248179
Tel:0135-2632380, 2632360

Howard International
The Mall,
Mussoorie-248179
Tel:0135-2632110, 2632105, 2632093

Shiva Continental
The Mall, Kulri
Mussoorie
Tel:0135-2632174,
Fax: 0135-2632780

Valley View Hotel
The Mall,
Mussoorie
Tel: 0135-2632174/2632211

Hotel Brentwood
Kulri
Mussoorie-248179
Tel: 0135-2632126, 2632036
Fax: 0135-2632604

Nainital

Nainital Club
Tel: 05942-235420

PWD Inspection House
Tel: 05942-235572

KMVN Tourist Rest House
Mallital
Tel: 05942-236897

KMVN TRC Snow View
Tel: 05942-235772

KMVN TRC
Tallital
Tel: 05942-235570

Hotel Arif Castle
Mallital
Tel: 05942-236005
Fax: 05942-236231

Balrampur House
Tel: 05942-236236
Fax: 05942-235103

Claridges Naini Retreat
Tel: 05942-235105
Fax: 05942-235103

Grand Hotel
The Mall
Tel: 05942-235406
Fax: 05942-237057

Belvedere Palace,
Awagarh Estate
Tel: 05042-235082

Shervani Hilltop Inn
Tel: 05942-236128
Fax: 05942-236304

Munsiyari

Zara Resort
Tel: 059612-2239

KMVN Tourist Rest House
Tel: 059612-22524

Narendra Nagar

Ananda –In the Himalayas,
The Palace Estate, Narendra Nagar
Tel: 01378-227500
Fax: 01378-227550
Email: sales@anandaspa.com

Ramnagar

Claridges Corbett Hideaway
Zero Gargia, Dhikuli
Ram Nagar, Uttranchal-244 715
Tel: 05947-284132, 284134
Delhi: Tel: 011-26413304, 26293905, 26293906
Fax: 011-26413303

Corbett Riverside Resort
Tel: 05947-287926, 287925
Delhi: Tel: 011-26560665, 26565191
Fax: 011-26565191

Tiger Camp, Dhikuli
Tel: 05947-287901/287902
Noida: Tel: 95120-24551963, 24524874
Fax: 011-29394878

The Corbett Inn, Ramnagar
Tel: 011-26934236, 26934237
Fax: 011-26934237

Ranikhet

Hotel Meghdoot
The Mall
Tel:05966-220475

Hotel West View
The Mall
Tel: 05966-220261
Delhi: 011-2648598, 26429790

Norton's Hotel
The Mall
Tel: 05966-220377

KMVN Tourist Rest House
The Mall
Tel: 05966-220893

Central Reservations from KMVN
HQ: 05942-236356
Fax: 236374

Moon Hotel
Sadar Bazaar
Tel: 05966-20382
Delhi: 011-27258466, 22523172

Hotel Raj Deep
Sadar Bazaar
Tel: 05966-20447

Parvati Inn
Sadar Bazaar
Tel: 05966-20325

Pauri

GMVN Tourist Rest House
Tel: 01368-222359

Circuit House

Forest Rest House

Soldier's Board Rest House

Hotel Sun & Snow
Tel: 01368-22242, 222466

Hotel Himalaya
Tel: 01368-226466

Hotel Frontier
Tel: 01368-222270

Pithoragarh

Rudra Tourist Complex
Tel: 01364-233347

PWD Inspection House

Pushdeep Hotel

Uttarakhand Tourist Lodge

Hotel New Tourist

Hotel Devlok

Indralok Hotel

Badri-Kedar Tourist Lodge

Hotel Poonam

Jeet Tourist Lodge

Dev Bhumi Tourist Lodge

Prayag Raj Hotel

Surya Lodge

Pinaki Hill Resort

Krishna Lodge

Dobhal Lodge

Dev Darshan Lodge

Tehri

PWD Inspection House

River View Hotel

New Krishna Hotel

Tourist Hotel

Paryatak Vishram Grih

Uttarkashi

PWD Inspection House
Tel:01374-2108

Forest Rest House
Tel: 01374-22444

Nim Rest House
Tel: 01374-22123

Tourist Rest House
Tel: 01374-22271

Travelers Lodge
Tel: 01374-22222

Bhandari Hotel
Tel: 01374-22203

Laxmi Hotel
Tel: 01374-22276

Joshi Lodge
Tel: 01374-2323

Shekhar Hotel
Tel: 01374-22170
Vijay Raj Hotel
Tel: 01374-22334

Mandakini Hotel
Tel: 01374-23337

Relax Hotel
Tel: 01374-22893

Yuv Raj Hotel
Tel: 01374-22008

Shivam Hotel
Tel: 01374-22880

Gomukh Hotel
Tel: 01374-22352

Hari Om Hotel
Tel: 01374-22328

Sahaj Villa
Tel: 01374-22783

Neel Kanth Hotel
Tel: 01374-22544

Amba Hotel
Tel: 01374-22646

Kapoor Hotel
Tel: 01374-22420

Miscellaneous: Binsar, Bhimtal, Chamba, Chaukori, Kanatal, Mukteshwar, Naukuchiya Tal, Ramgarh, Sat Tal, Sitlakhet

Binsar
Mountain Resort
Tel: 05962-251011
Fax: 05962-51048, 31700

KMVN Tourist Rest House
Tel: 05962-251010

Bhimtal
Country Inn
Tel/Fax: 05942-247017

KMVN Tourist Rest House
Tel: 05942-247005

Chamba
Classic Hill Top Resort
Mussoorie Road
Arakot
Tel:01376-255252

Chaukori
KMVN Tourist Rest House

Kanatal
The Hermitage Hotel
Tel: 011-26421322/32323
Fax: 011-26833298
Email: kanatal@hotmail.com

Mukteshwar
Camp Purple
Tel: 011-26850492
Fax: 011-26533212
Email: wildrfit@vsnl.com

Mountain Trail
Tel: 05942-288040, 288240
Fax: 011-267652024

KMVN Tourist Rest House

Naukuchiya Tal
Eurotel Parichay
Tel: 05942-247041
Fax: 05942-23364

The Lake Resort
Tel: 05942-247183, 84

KMVN Tourist Rest House

Ramgarh
Hotel Roop Kumaon
Tel: 05942-281200, 20, 21
Writers Bungalow
Email:salesneemrana.com

Cedar Lodge
Malla Ramgarh
Tel: 05947-281154, 284125/26
Tel: 011-26560665
Fax: 011-26565191
Email:nainaahmad@yahoo.com

The Ramgarh Bungalows
Malla Ramgarh
Tel: 05942-281156/37

KMVN Tourist Rest House

Sat Tal
KMVN Rest House
Tel: 05942-47047

Saat-Taal Camp
Tel:011-26850492, 26963342

Fax: 011-26533212
Email: wildrfit@vsnl.com

Sitlakhet
Tourist Rest House, Sitlakhet
Tel: 05962-6005

Udham Singh Nagar

Irrigation Dept Inspection House

Forest Rest House

PWD Inspection House

Hotel Kanchantara
Tel: 05944-283969

Hotel Sonia
Tel: 05944-283883

Hotel Suvidha
Tel: 05944-283747

Hotel Mid Town
Tel: 05944-284762

Hotel Prince
Tel: 05944-284253

Hotel Mansarovar
Tel: 05944-281820

Hotel Era
Tel: 05944-285648

Hotel Mani Palace
Tel: 05944-284483

Hotel Siddhu Palace
Tel: 05944-28195

IMPORTANT NOTES